As one of the world's longest established
and best-known travel brands,
Thomas Cook are the experts in travel.

For more than 135 years our
guidebooks have unlocked the secrets
of destinations around the world,
sharing with travellers a wealth of
experience and a passion for travel.

**Rely on Thomas Cook as your
travelling companion on your next trip
and benefit from our unique heritage.**

Thomas Cook **traveller** guides

MADEIRA
Christopher Catling

Thomas
Cook

Your travelling companion since 1873

Written by Christopher Catling, updated by Gordon Lethbridge
Original photography by Jon Wyand

Published by Thomas Cook Publishing
A division of Thomas Cook Tour Operations Limited.
Company registration no. 3772199 England
The Thomas Cook Business Park, Unit 9, Coningsby Road,
Peterborough PE3 8SB, United Kingdom
Email: books@thomascook.com, Tel: + 44 (0) 1733 416477
www.thomascookpublishing.com

Produced by Cambridge Publishing Management Limited
Burr Elm Court, Main Street, Caldecote CB23 7NU

ISBN: 978-1-84848-220-3

Series Editor: Maisie Fitzpatrick
Production/DTP: Steven Collins

Printed and bound in Italy by Printer Trento

Cover photography: © Pictures Colour Library

Contents

Introduction

It has been said that if you do not have time to visit the world you should visit Madeira. Imagine what it would be like to have a bit of all the best parts of the world in one place, add in some European culture and you have the Madeiran archipelago. However, Madeira is more than the sum of its parts; it has an identity that is also unique.

The islands of the Madeiran archipelago are a fascinating blend of contrasting and unlikely ingredients, places that remind you of other far-flung destinations, while remaining uniquely themselves. H N Coleridge wrote in 1825 that Madeira... 'ensures almost every European comfort together with almost every tropical luxury'.

The steep terraced hillsides with their burgeoning banana crops may put you in mind of Bali or the Philippines; English roses and perennials grow in profusion alongside Asian orchids and Indian tulip trees; the island's fragrant eucalyptus woods recall Australia, while the gorse-covered moorlands of the central plateau could be in the Scottish Highlands.

The architecture of Madeira's capital evokes yet another place and time – the elegant balconies and shaded patios of Funchal seem straight out of the half-real, half-imaginary world of an Isabel Allende or Gabriel García Márquez novel, while its streets depict paving patterns with a more modern aesthetic.

On top of all this, Madeira encompasses spectacular ravines and waterfalls, ever-changing skies and seas, and mountain tops where you can enjoy a rare sense of stillness and peace as you admire the magnificent panoramas.

Bustling Funchal is also part of Madeira's rich texture and it is a pleasure to return to the capital at the end of a long day's tour, knowing that you can look forward to all the modern comforts of a luxurious hotel and the prospect of an excellent dinner – with or without a glass or two of Madeira, the island's fortified wine.

Nature's profusion is all the more enjoyable when accompanied by such civilised comforts, and that is why Madeira is such a delightful and satisfying holiday destination.

Walking the island's *levadas* and visiting its gardens, observing its wealth of folk traditions and customs and meeting its hospitable and easy-going people, will provide a complete change of scene.

Villages nestle under high mountain peaks

The land

Madeira is a tiny island set in the Atlantic Ocean, a long way from anywhere. The nearest mainland is the coast of Morocco, 608km (378 miles) away. It is even further to Portugal, the country to which Madeira belongs, for the capital, Lisbon, is nearly 1,000km (620 miles) to the northeast.

Yet Madeira is not entirely alone: it is partnered by the smaller island of Porto Santo, 37km (23 miles) to the northeast, a popular summertime destination for Madeirans because of its long beach and golden sands. Another group of islands, the Ilhas Desertas (Deserted Isles), lies 16km (10 miles) to the southeast and is usually visible from Funchal. The islands live up to their name by being uninhabited except for birds, seals and visiting naturalists. Much more distant, and also uninhabited, are the Ilhas Selvagens ('Wild Islands'), which lie 216km (134 miles) to the south; they also belong to the Madeiran archipelago, even though they are closer to the Spanish-owned Canary Islands.

The terrain

Madeira is about the same size as Singapore, but beyond that all comparisons cease. You could drive the length of flat Singapore in under an hour, but the same journey would take up to half a day on mountainous Madeira. Distances are magnified by the steepness of the terrain. From the island's main east–west mountain range, numerous high ridges run north and south to the coast. Most roads have to take a tortuous zigzagging route in order to negotiate the deep valleys and ravines that lie in between. This type of contorted terrain was very aptly described in a 19th-century guidebook which recounted a meeting between Christopher Columbus and Queen Isabella of Spain. The queen asked Columbus to describe Jamaica to her. He picked up a piece of paper, crumpled it between his hands and put it down again, saying 'This will give you a better idea of the island's appearance than any of my words'. Precisely the same will do for Madeira.

Another antiquated guidebook describes Madeira poetically as 'surrounded by an abysmal ocean'. The truth of this is brought home as you tour the island, especially the northern

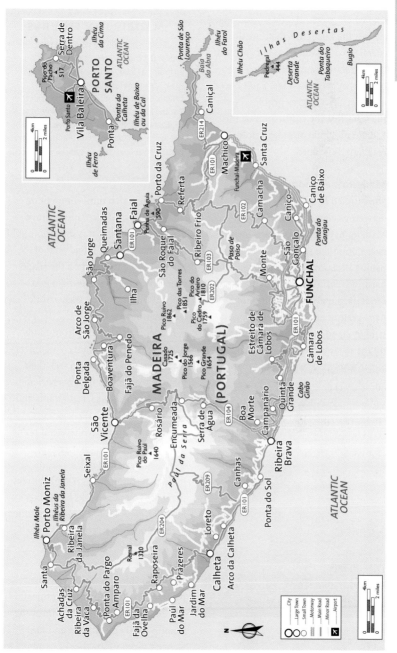

side where great Atlantic waves break against the high cliffs that line this coast. Sea and land meet abruptly on the island, with no gently shelving beaches in between – just a jumble of jagged rocks and grey pebbles. Below the waterline the cliffs continue for 1,000m (3,300ft) or more before reaching the seabed.

Madeira's economy

Surrounded by such a deep and dangerous element, the people of Madeira have tended to turn their backs upon the sea, and the island's tiny fishing fleets employ only a handful of hardy adventurers. Instead, most Madeirans make their living from the hard graft of agriculture, tending the land by hand because there is no space on the narrow terraces for machinery. Sugar, known as 'white gold', made the

MADEIRA IN FIGURES

Population: 245,000 (of whom 86 per cent live on the sunny south of the island, including 115,000 in the capital, Funchal).
Area: 738sq km (285sq miles).
Length: 56km (35 miles) east to west.
Width: 23km (14 miles) north to south.
Highest point: Pico Ruivo (1,862m/6,109ft).
Sea depth: 6,000m (19,700ft) in the Canary Basin, which lies 83km (52 miles) to the west of Madeira.

early settlers rich until competition from New World plantations drove prices down. Today it is the yellow gold of bananas and the liquid gold of Madeira wine that sustain the island economy, along with tourism and handicrafts, including wickerwork and embroidery.

Madeira also benefits from funds from so-called 'emigrants' – islanders who have gone abroad to seek their fortune working in the Venezuelan oil industry, or in shops, restaurants and hotels in Britain, South Africa or Australia. The money they send home to help their families is a very significant element in the island's invisible economy and it explains why there are so many banks based in Funchal, competing against each other for the emigrants' accounts.

Climate

Madeira is blessed with an almost perfect climate – it is never intolerably hot and never too cold. In winter, the island's southerly latitude and the warmth given off by the sea combine to

The drama of Madeira's volcanic peaks is enhanced by the play of the elements

The shimmer of a rainbow perfects a picture-postcard landscape

ensure that temperatures do not often dip below a pleasant 18°C (64°F). This makes Madeira a popular destination for anyone seeking an escape from the icy grip of northern European winters.

In summer, the trade winds help to keep Madeira cool, and clouds build up to screen the island from the hot midday sunshine so temperatures rarely exceed 24°C (75°F). This makes Madeira a popular destination for mainland Portuguese visitors, along with anyone else fleeing the searing heat of continental summers (by contrast, Madeirans themselves, looking for some really hot sunshine for a change, go and roast themselves on neighbouring Porto Santo, which in summer is usually very hot and dry).

Despite the equable nature of Madeira's climate, there is also great variety: temperatures drop rapidly with altitude, and chill winds can blow on the mountain tops even in summer; that is why the stallholders who sell sweaters on the top of Pico do Arieiro (1,810m/5,938ft) enjoy a brisk trade.

In winter you can often enjoy the experience of playing with snowballs on the mountain peaks in the morning and sunbathing by the hotel pool in the afternoon.

Even more enthralling is to walk among the high peaks of Madeira in brilliant sunshine, while below you cottonwool clouds shroud the island.

Rain can be guaranteed to freshen up every day – only in July and August is it likely to be dry. Fortunately, in Funchal, the rainfall tends to come in short bursts: after a clear start to the day, clouds build up and there is often a downpour by noon, so that the late afternoon and evening are clear and sunny once again.

History

20 million years ago Volcanic eruptions under the Atlantic build up layers of lava to create the Madeiran islands.

1.7 million years ago Madeiran volcanoes become extinct. Volcanic soils nurture the woodland that cloaks the island.

2,000 years ago Though known to Phoenician, Roman and North African sailors, the uninhabited islands are never colonised.

1418 One of the many expeditions sponsored by Prince Henry 'The Navigator' (son of King João I of Portugal) is blown off course by violent storms. Captain João Gonçalves Zarco finds shelter off an island which he names Porto Santo (Blessed Port) in gratitude.

1420 Returning to explore, Zarco discovers what he calls Ilha da Madeira, the Island of Wood.

1425 Settlement begins in earnest. Early settlers grow rich producing 'white gold' – sugar cane.

1452 The first slaves are brought from Africa and the Canaries to build Madeira's terraces, dig the irrigation channels and work the fields.

1478 Christopher Columbus visits Madeira to buy sugar. He later marries Filipa Moniz, daughter of Bartolomeu Perestrello, first governor of Porto Santo.

1542 The defensive walls around Funchal are built as protection from pirates.

1566 1,000 French pirates attack Funchal.

1580 Philip II of Spain occupies Portugal, and Madeira comes under Spanish rule.

1640 The Portuguese revolt against Spanish rule, and regain their independence under King João IV.

1662 Catherine of Braganza, daughter of King João IV, marries Charles II of England. Granted commercial privileges, English merchants settle on Madeira, dominating the Madeira wine trade.

1775	Slavery is declared illegal in Portugal.
1803	Flash floods inundate Funchal: 600 are drowned. The city's three rivers are enclosed by high walls to prevent future disasters.
1807–13	British troops garrisoned on Madeira to prevent Napoleon invading.
1852	Cholera carries off 7,000 victims, and the island's vineyards are devastated by mildew.
1887	Economy is boosted by European tourists visiting for the winter, or staying en route to South America and the Far East.
1931	Troops from Lisbon are used to put down a general strike protesting against the regime of the Portuguese dictator, Salazar. Madeirans begin emigrating in large numbers in search of a better life.
1964	First commercial flights from Santa Catarina.

1974	Portugal enters a new era of democracy.
1976	Madeira becomes an autonomous region, with a regional government and president.
1986	Portugal's entry into the European Community gives Madeira access to development funds.
1997–2000	The island's south-coast expressway transforms life on the island.
2000	João Jardim is elected president for the sixth time.
2002	Madeira adopts the euro.
2007	New Year Firework Display enters *Guinness World Records* as the largest firework display.
2009	The International Whaling Commission holds its Annual General Meeting in Funchal marking Madeira's transformation from a whaling nation to a whale conservation nation. Former President Dr Néuo Mendonça dies.
2010	Atlantic Festival (fireworks display) takes place in June.

The colonisation of Madeira

Madeira had no indigenous population when Zarco landed in 1420, but the island soon attracted Flemish, Italian, Spanish, French and English adventurers. Many came as merchants who invested in land and made fortunes from sugar cultivation and the wine trade. English involvement in the island increased substantially after Charles II married Catherine of Braganza, daughter of King João IV of Portugal, in 1662. England very nearly gained Madeira as part of Catherine's dowry; it is said that the scribe who drew up the marriage contract was Madeiran and that patriotism led him to omit the island. English traders moved in anyway when Charles II passed a law in 1665 prohibiting the export of European goods to the English colonies in America, unless they were shipped through English ports in English ships. Madeira was explicitly excluded from this restriction, and one result was the rapid growth of wine shipments from the island to the colonies. The Americans grew to like Madeira wine so much that it was used to toast the signing of the Declaration of Independence in 1776. The lucrative trade also helped establish some of the island's oldest merchant families, such as the Blandys and the Leacocks, who are still very much in business today.

Foreign tourists have also had a major impact on the island, whether coming for the good of their health, or escaping from the cold northern European winter, or stopping en route to India, the Far East, South Africa or South America. Only the wealthy could afford to come to Madeira, hence the genteel upmarket image which still prevails today, though this has been eroded somewhat by mass-market tourism, following the extension of the airport runway in 1985 and the large-scale development of the Hotel and Tourist zones of Funchal.

Porto Moniz: visitors benefit from Madeira's climate and clean air

Sightseeing olden style, by hammock

Politics

The winds of political change came late to Madeira. Until 1968, it had to endure the totalitarian regime of the Portuguese dictator, António de Oliveira Salazar. Salazar's successor, the marginally more liberal prime minister, Caetano, was then deposed in the Carnation Revolution of 1974: the military took control but symbolised their desire for peaceful change by carrying flowers in their gun barrels.

Creating a new democracy

At the time of the 1974 revolution there were many in Madeira who wanted complete independence from Portugal. This reaction was understandable – during the long years of the Salazar regime, Madeirans were made to feel as if they were helpless inhabitants of a remote little island who would be lost without mother Portugal. At the beginning of every day, Madeiran schoolchildren were made to repeat: *A nação é tudo; tudo pela nação* (the nation is all; all to the nation). This fine-sounding slogan was used to disguise an ugly truth: the Lisbon government had been milking the Madeiran economy for decades, appropriating revenues from exports and tourism, so that what should have been a prosperous island was left with some of the worst poverty and deprivation in Europe.

Politically active Madeirans were determined that islanders should in future be in charge of their own destiny; they were eventually persuaded that it might be better to remain part of Portugal, but as an autonomous region. This means that Madeira now controls its own economy and sets its own taxes and customs duties as well as deciding how much should be spent on health, welfare and educational programmes. The island still looks to the Portuguese mainland for its foreign and defence policies, and the brightest Madeiran students still go to Portugal for their university education, but since 1974 there has been a growing sense of island identity; the people of Madeira are proud of their history and culture and now tend to think of themselves as Madeirans first and Portuguese second.

The system of government

Madeira, Porto Santo and the other islands of the archipelago make up what Madeiran newspapers call the RAM (Região Autónoma da Madeira). This is governed by the 50-seat regional parliament, based in Funchal, which has the power to pass legislation and deal with all issues directly affecting the islands. In practice, many of the day-to-day decisions are taken by the executive committee, consisting of the president, the vice-president and six secretaries. The island also has a number of town councils responsible for more local issues and, on a broader stage, Madeira elects five representatives from the regional parliament who sit as members of the Lisbon-based Portuguese parliament.

Parties and personalities

Madeira's head of state since 1978 has been Dr Alberto João Jardim, an extremely popular and charismatic figure whose picture appears almost daily on the front page of Madeiran newspapers as he cuts the ribbon to inaugurate a new school or health clinic. President Jardim's PSD (Popular Social Democrat) party holds most of the seats in the regional parliament and regularly polls 70 per cent of the vote in elections, which are held every four years.

Dissent, such as it is, centres around the PS (Socialist) party and the right-of-centre CDS. The smaller parties are better represented at town council level, and it is here that a conflict of policies occasionally takes place. It is hard, though, for opposition parties to dent President Jardim's popularity because he has presided over decades of unprecedented growth, during which the living standard of most Madeirans

has improved very substantially. Today, most villages have electricity, schools and a health clinic, as well as a road link to the capital, Funchal, all of which were just a politician's dream in the 1970s.

Now Madeira's problems are concerned with the consequences of rapid growth, including pollution, uncontrolled building and abandonment of the land resulting from Madeira's greater prosperity.

Jardim resigned in February 2007 in protest at the Portuguese government's 2007 budget which reduced funding for the archipelago. Somewhat predictably, he was re-elected to the post almost immediately, the whole affair proving just how popular and powerful a figure he is on the island.

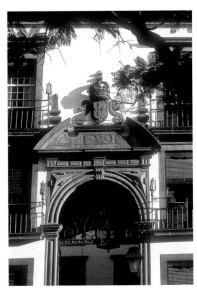

Government offices in Funchal

Tales of discovery

Many stories have been told about the discovery and colonisation of Madeira, and many myths persist to this day. One is that Madeira is the last vestige of the drowned continent of Atlantis; another is that the lost treasure of the notorious pirate Captain Kidd is buried on one of the Ilhas Selvagens.

The truth is more prosaic. It is known for a fact that the Madeiran islands were familiar to navigators long before Porto Santo and Madeira were officially 'discovered' by João Gonçalves Zarco in 1418 and 1420.

Pliny, the 1st-century AD Roman writer, called them the 'Purple Islands' because of the distinctive colour of Madeira's volcanic rocks and soil. The Medici map of 1351, drawn by Genoese cartographers, was the first to depict Madeira and give it a name – Isola delle Lolegname (Island of Wood). The same name – Ilha da Madeira in Portuguese – was used by Zarco when he landed in 1420, laying claim to the island on behalf of Portugal.

The story of Robert Machin

Facts, though, are rarely as romantic as the tales embroidered by sailors with time on their hands as they sailed the Atlantic carrying cargoes of Madeiran sugar, grain and wine. About 100 years after Zarco's discovery, chronicler Valentine Fernandes published a different account, which he no doubt heard in some harbourside bar. This concerns a Bristol merchant, Robert Machin, who was blown out into the Atlantic by a storm while sailing to Portugal. Ending up within sight of Madeira, Machin went ashore to investigate. His mutinous crew decided to abandon Machin, but they got caught up in another storm which drove them on to the Moroccan coast where they were taken prisoner, destined to serve as galley slaves.

Determined to return to civilisation, Machin built himself a raft. He, too, fell prey to Moroccan pirates and ended up in the same prison as his former crew. Machin then furiously attacked one of his fellow sailors, meaning to kill him in revenge. Astonished by the ferocity of the fight, Machin's gaolers forced him to explain his actions and it was not long before the whole story of the mysterious island at the edge of the known world began to circulate. It was only a matter of time before Henry the Navigator heard the story and sent Zarco out to investigate.

Even more romantic versions of Machin's story circulated in the 17th century in which he is portrayed as an English aristocrat eloping with his sweetheart, Anna d'Arfet (or Anne of Hertford).

Shipwrecked on Madeira, she dies of exposure and he of a broken heart. Zarco is said to have found their graves when he stepped ashore in 1420, inspiring him to name the spot Machico. Another Madeiran legend has it that Zarco set fire to Madeira – this being the fastest way to clear the island's dense woodland – and that the forests blazed for seven years.

In fact, clearance was probably much more selective: the island's timber was a valuable resource, used for building houses, ships and the crates to hold sugar and other crops.

Columbus and Madeira

Another colourful and persistent story has it that Christopher Columbus lived on both Madeira and Porto Santo for several years; here he married, fathered his only son, and became convinced by the exotic plant remains washed up on Madeira's shores that sailing westward would bring him to the spice islands of the Indies. He therefore sailed back to Lisbon determined to raise funds for an expedition to test his theory.

The story sounds too neat, too well honed to be true, and for many years the Madeirans themselves were among the most sceptical.

Nowadays, however, it looks as if the legend may contain some truth, and that Columbus may have even returned to live on Madeira, off and on, after his discovery of the New World.

For the 1992 quincentenary celebrations, Madeirans decided to acknowledge and capitalise on the Columbus connection for the first time, and visitors to Porto Santo (*pp132–7*) can now visit the Casa de Colombo (House of Columbus) museum, with its portraits of the great man and early maps of Madeira and the Americas.

Columbus's house on Porto Santo

Culture

Madeira is an island in transition from third-world levels of poverty to first-world prosperity. The change, not yet complete, has nevertheless been so rapid that you can simultaneously glimpse scenes from Madeira's past and from its future as you tour the island.

Driving into the village of Santana, for example, you are quite likely to catch sight of what looks like a walking haystack – a peasant farmer invisible beneath the great stack of hay that she is carrying to feed her cow. She and her family may well live in a traditional thatched A-framed house and cook in the open air over a wood fire. She may wash herself and her clothes in a nearby *levada* (irrigation canal), and the family may survive on an income of around €5,000 a year. Her husband will work tiny terraced fields by hand and will think nothing of carrying the produce he grows in wicker baskets – for very long distances along steep and winding mountain paths – to the roadside for the local co-operative to collect.

Roads and change

Until recently there were still villages and farms on the island that were two hours' arduous walk from the nearest road, that had no electricity or television and where some of the inhabitants had never travelled to see the island's capital, Funchal.

The number of Madeirans who live this traditional life – spending all their waking hours in laborious work without the benefit of modern technology – has dwindled rapidly in recent years. Road-building programmes, partly funded by European Union grants, have been a major catalyst for change. As new roads have been driven further into the remotest parts of Madeira's interior, electricity has followed, generated by wind turbines located on the island's northern cliffs and the Paúl da Serra plateau, or by water turbines powered by the outflow from reservoirs. Roads mean that farmers can drive their crops to the agricultural co-operative or sell direct to hotels and restaurants. Many now travel to Funchal every Friday to sell their produce in the lively Mercado dos Lavradores (Workers' Market).

As villages have been linked into the island's road network, the land-hungry have arrived: urbanites looking for plots on which to build a weekend home and emigrants returning from overseas with a nest egg looking for somewhere to build a retirement home. To the despair of those who love the island's traditional architecture and natural beauty, many scenic villages are now almost surrounded by newly built villas, and the green hillsides splattered with bright orange roof tiles and white walls. To complete the transformation, tourists can now reach almost every corner of the island by coach, taxi or hire car, and shops, restaurants and even hotels have been opened to cater for them. Many villages have benefited from a general increase in prosperity.

Town and country

It is difficult to predict what long-term effect these changes will have on the culture of Madeira, although Funchal offers some clues as to how the rest of the island may develop. The Catholic Church, which is still a major force in the lives of rural Madeirans, has far less power in the capital – so much so that many parish churches in Funchal are locked and unused. Where religious processions to honour the Virgin or a patron saint draw crowds of devotees in the villages, only events such as the New Year festivities and the Madeira Wine Rally attract similar numbers in the city.

The Funchalese see themselves as sophisticated and cosmopolitan, intellectual and, where religion is concerned, at best agnostic. Yet loyalty to the family remains as strong as ever it was and the people of Funchal are every bit as hardworking and entrepreneurial as their country cousins. What is more, there is a strong sense of pride in the things that make Madeira special and unique – its wines, landscapes and architecture, and even the traditional dances and costumes, which are performed and worn for pleasure and not merely to earn tourist revenue.

A wall plaque illustrates a scene now rarely witnessed – carrying produce to market the old way

Festivals

If one goes by the pervasive air of celebration, almost every day seems to be a festival day on Madeira. But festivals are still announced in the traditional way, by setting off a string of explosive firecrackers and shooting rockets into the air. In the days before telephone, post or newspapers, this was an effective way of inviting your neighbours to come across and join in the fun.

Most village festivals (called *arraiais*) are rooted in the Catholic religion and are held to honour the local patron saint or to celebrate a major event in the church calendar – the Feast of the Assumption (15 August) is one of the biggest, and local celebrations often begin a full fortnight in advance of the day itself.

On the day itself, Mass is said, followed by processions of children and villagers dressed in their best, singing hymns. For visitors, such festivals offer the chance of sampling local wine and *espetada* kebabs cooked over the embers of a vinewood fire.

Other festivals and events are more formal and, with one eye to tourism, have been elaborated in recent years to increase their appeal to visitors. Here is a list of the main events to look out for:

January
Madeira Islands Walking Festival is an organised group walking programme in mid-January each year. A total of 20 walks, led by experienced and licensed guides, are on offer over five days along the island's *levadas* and trails, which range in difficulty and length.

February
Carnival is celebrated in villages all over the island, but the costumed parades held in Funchal are the best. The parade, held on the Saturday before Shrove Tuesday, features satirical floats poking mild fun at the authorities, accompanied by bands and fireworks, while a second parade on Shrove Tuesday itself features clowns and fancy dress.

April/May
Madeira's **Flower Festival**, held on a weekend at the end of April or early in May, sees Funchal transformed into a blaze of colour. Streets, houses, shop windows and churches are decorated with ribbons, flags, floral carpets and pictures made of flowers. The climax is a parade of flower-smothered floats through the city's main streets.

June

The Atlantic Festival has three components: the Music Festival, the International Fireworks Competition and street entertainment that includes street musicians, jugglers and other acts.

The Music Festival allows visitors and residents to enjoy high-quality classical music in some of Madeira's best examples of its architectural heritage.

Every Saturday evening for three weekends the best pyrotechnic companies in the world put on a music and fireworks show in a bid to win the coveted prize of putting on the prestigious New Year display later in the year.

August

Car fanatics regard the **Madeira Wine Rally** as one of the toughest stages of the European championships. If you are in Funchal for the start of the rally in early August you will hear the ear-ripping sound of the rally-car engines.

Madeira's biggest religious festival takes place on 15 August, when devout Catholics from all over the island visit Our Lady's church at Monte (*see pp69 & 72*), climbing the steps to the church on their knees, to honour the **Assumption of the Virgin Mary**.

September

Wine festivals in Funchal and Câmara de Lobos feature wine tasting, dancing in the streets and demonstrations of grape treading (*see pp70–71*).

December

Christmas preparations begin as early as 8 December when *bolo de mel* (honey cake) is traditionally made and when children plant wheat, maize or barley seeds in small pots. About ten days later the pots begin to sprout a head of fresh green shoots, symbolising renewal and plenty in the year ahead. The pots are placed round the crib figures. From 8 December, Funchal's streets are lit up nightly with coloured bulbs and illuminations, in preparation for the island's spectacular **New Year's Eve** festival (*see pp22–3*).

Decorating the streets in preparation for Madeira's spring flower festival

New Year

New Year on Madeira is the climax of the island's festive calendar. From 8 December, the city of Funchal will have been ablaze every night, with nearly half a million coloured bulbs outlining the shapes of buildings, draped over trees, and illuminating the waterfront promenade. As New Year approaches, Madeiran emigrants from South America, Australia, Canada and southern Africa fly home to be with their families, joining the hundreds of tourists who jet in to enjoy the warmth of a Madeiran Christmas, and the many sea voyagers – in small boats and in huge luxury liners – who all set sail for Funchal's harbour.

On New Year's Eve itself another migration begins as Madeirans from all over the island head for Funchal in cars, trucks and buses, clogging all the approach roads. The aim of all this movement is to be in Funchal for a spectacular fireworks display put on by the winner of the International Fireworks Competition held during the Atlantic Festival earlier in the year. The display earned an entry in *Guinness World Records 2007* as the biggest in the world. As midnight approaches on New Year's Eve, the lights are turned on in every building in Funchal and its suburbs, doors are opened and curtains drawn open so that the whole amphitheatre of hills enclosing the city seems a blaze of lights, matched by the lights of the ships and boats in the harbour. Silence falls, and then, as the bewitching hour strikes, all Funchal explodes with the sound of ships' sirens, the popping of champagne corks, church bells ringing, and the cheers of onlookers, all accompanied by a meteor storm of coloured rockets bursting overhead. Those who have seen it once regularly return, which is why hotel rates double over the Christmas and New Year period – if you want to be there yourself, be certain to book at least a year in advance.

Brightly lit ships host parties in the harbour

Champagne corks and fireworks all reach for the sky at midnight on New Year

Impressions

When Zarco first caught sight of Madeira in 1420 it was covered in cloud and he thought he was approaching the edge of the world – the place where, according to medieval cosmography, demons and evil spirits dwelt. By the time he landed he had changed his view entirely and rapturously described the island as a place of 'lightsome beauty... the land of fairies'.

Today's traveller, arriving by air, still experiences a sense of journeying across endless ocean until the jewel-like island, intensely green and set in a crystal clear blue sea, suddenly appears on the horizon. All too quickly that vision is lost as you descend to Madeira's international airport and are whisked off, with great efficiency, through the Funchal traffic to your hotel.

Once you have settled into the hotel, it is easy to be seduced into spending all week by the poolside, strolling through the streets of Funchal, or lingering for hours over lunch in some harbourside seafood restaurant. It is easy to forget that glimpse you had of the green mountains rising out of the sea – all too easy, in fact, to become part of that statistic that says 80 per cent of Madeira's visitors do not travel beyond the confines of Funchal. That would be a pity, because the island's coastal and mountain landscapes are some of the most spectacular in Europe; moreover,

they are also very accessible by coach tour, public bus or taxi.

Planning your time

The best strategy for enjoying the real Madeira is to spend the first day or so unwinding and getting to know Funchal; then take a tour on the second or third day of your stay.

Too many people leave seeing the island until the last moment, signing up for a round-the-island tour towards the end of their visit, only to discover what pleasures they have missed all week. Nor does it make sense to try to see all of Madeira in a day: a typical island tour covers 150km (93 miles), most of the day spent in a coach, yet covering only a fraction of the island's varied charms.

It is far better to split Madeira into two, and visit the western and eastern sides separately. Most tour operators operate the two separate tours on different days, which allows you to see the two contrasting sides of Madeira by coach, minibus or covered jeep.

Impressions

If you are travelling with a tour operator, remember that while their excursions are a bit more expensive than those offered on the street, the extra few euros guarantee you only one language on the coach.

Remember, too, that the skies are often clearer in the morning than the afternoon, and while there is always risk of cloud, mist or rain during the day, the views may be far better if you take a pre-lunch rather than post-lunch tour.

Taxis: how to get a good rate

Many tour operators will also organise taxi excursions for you, which is actually preferable to negotiating directly with the taxi drivers themselves.

A good tour operator will be able to find you a reliable taxi driver who will drive carefully (it is easy enough to suffer from travel sickness or vertigo on Madeira's steep and winding roads), who knows the island thoroughly, and who speaks English (or any other language) fluently.

Taxis can usually be hired by the half-day (9am–1pm or 1–5pm) or the full day. The rates are supposed to be fixed by the taxi drivers' association, but beware of drivers who try to charge more.

If only two people are sharing a taxi, then the cost will be slightly higher than if they take a coach tour, but if three or more people are sharing the price of the taxi, then the taxi fare works out cheaper.

The beautiful view over Madeira's airport

Praça do Município, Funchal's main square

Touts

Madeira is remarkably free, so far at least, of timeshare touts and similar nuisances, but they do exist, and it is best to be forewarned. Timeshare touts are paid large sums of money to get you to sign an irrevocable and expensive contract, and they will use every tactic possible to get you to do so. These touts tend to hang around the Hotel Zone, but a firm 'no' usually gets rid of them.

Thanks to the large number of returning holidaymakers with high disposable incomes, timeshare has taken off in a large way over the last few years, with most of the new five-star hotels selling up to 30 per cent of their rooms on a 30-year timeshare basis.

Instead of dealing with touts, it is better to contact reputable companies –

for instance, Porto Bay, owner of three hotels on the island, and Pestana, the largest hotel owner in Portugal. These two companies have new flagship properties for both normal hotel bookings and timeshare ownership, and are building more.

Avoid unlicensed drivers offering tours or taxi services as they charge exorbitant rates.

THOMAS COOK'S MADEIRA

The first reference to a Cook's holiday to Madeira was in 1885, when the island was included as part of a trip to the Portuguese mainland. In the early 20th century, steamers, which resembled 'floating hotels', departed regularly from London and Liverpool to make round-trip cruises to Madeira, calling at the Canary Islands as well. In the *Traveller's Gazette*, in 1921, Madeira was described as 'this flower-bedecked isle under Ionian skies'.

The yellow licensed taxis operate with fixed or metered fares (*see p186*). Most taxi drivers are honest, but be wary of seeking their advice, especially on which restaurants are best. They will offer to take you somewhere good, cheap and typically Madeiran: and all too often that restaurant will be located so far out of town that you have to pay a higher taxi fare, and it will be at such a distance from any other restaurant that you will have no choice but to eat there. By the time you discover it is also twice as expensive as downtown restaurants, the driver will have disappeared (he will be back later to collect his commission from the restaurant owner).

If you are aware of these tricks, they are easy to avoid, and you should have a carefree, enjoyable holiday.

Madeira, 'the flower-bedecked isle'

Funchal

Madeira's capital is an elegant city, once dubbed 'little Lisbon' by visiting mariners because of the grandeur of its cathedral and harbourside buildings. The city resembles a huge amphitheatre sheltered by a semicircle of hills, with open views out across the harbour to the sea and the distant Ilhas Desertas.

Most of Madeira's hotels occupy elevated positions to the west of Funchal, built on the clifftops and hills to make the most of the views. From this Hotel Zone it takes up to 30 minutes to reach central Funchal on foot, or a few minutes by taxi. Madeirans themselves complain about traffic and pollution in the capital, and it's true that the diesel fumes can be oppressive during the morning and evening rush hours (around 9am and 5pm), but visitors from many other cities will consider Funchal delightfully quiet.

CENTRAL FUNCHAL

Funchal's main avenue, Avenida Arriaga, was laid out at the turn of the 20th century with a wide central carriageway, shaded by trees and equipped with benches, where Madeirans come to stroll and gossip, especially in the evenings. The avenue is lined with trees, gardens, fountains, fashionable shops, and belle époque mansions, now the prestigious premises of banks and government departments.

Traffic still uses the Avenida do Mar, the city's wide seafront promenade, but this is an ideal spot from which to admire the short but colourful Madeiran sunset, or for an after-dinner stroll. To the right of the avenue is the harbour area, where cruise ships are often docked.

This deep natural harbour helped Funchal edge out Machico, which rivalled Funchal in size and prosperity, to become the island capital. The great **Molhe da Pontinha**, the breakwater which surrounds the harbour, was built in 1895 and incorporates the tiny fortified island of **Loo Rock**, midway down its long concrete arm.

Work has started on converting the harbour to a leisure port. Cargo traffic has been moved to Santa Cruz and Machico and work started on a cruise ship terminal.

More fortifications survive to the landward side of Avenida do Mar, including the **Palácio de São Lourenço**. Bristling with cannons, it was built in the 1520s to defend the city against repeated pirate attacks, and later converted into the residence of the island's 19th-century governors, one civil and one military.

Following Avenida do Mar to its easternmost limit you will reach the Zona Velha, or Old Town (*see* The Old Town *walk, pp40–41*), with its narrow cobbled alleys and outdoor restaurants serving some of the best-value food to be had in the capital. Between the Hotel Zone and the Zona Velha lives the rest of the city (*see* Between the rivers *and* Elegant mansions *walks, pp32–3 & 56–7*), a wonderful jumble of modern and old, where stylish shops aimed at cruise passengers sit side by side with antiquated general stores selling daily necessities and smelling of salt cod and dried herbs.

The architecture is equally varied, and further colour is added by the many flower sellers and street traders who operate around the cathedral and **Mercado dos Lavradores** (or Workers' Market), itself a fascinating amalgam of sights and sounds.

To the west of the city, Estrada Monumental takes all the traffic leaving Funchal for the west of the island on to the new expressway linking Funchal to Ribeira Brava. Put up with the noise and try to enjoy the views towards

Funchal's deep natural harbour, with the Hotel Zone beyond

Funchal, which are especially good around Reid's Hotel.

In short, Funchal may be a small city, but it is not to be underestimated – each time you think you have covered every inch of the ground you will turn a corner and discover something entirely new.

Adegas de São Francisco

A visit to the Adegas de São Francisco (the St Francis Wine Lodge) is one of the most enjoyable ways to spend a couple of hours on Madeira, and if you are planning to take home a bottle or two of Madeira it is worth coming here first to learn about the history and production of this magnificent fortified wine.

The wine lodge is run by the Madeira Wine Company, a consortium whose shareholders include most of the famous names of the Madeira trade: Blandy, Leacock and Luiz Gomes. Everything about the lodge has the appropriate patina of time, and as soon (*Cont. on p34*)

CITY OF FENNEL

The name Funchal comes from *funcho*, meaning fennel. Zarco gave this name to the spot where he landed in July 1420 because of the abundance of the sweet-smelling herb that he found in flower.

Pavement patterns

It pays to look down wherever you walk in Funchal, to admire the style and craftsmanship of the humble pavements. In the Zona Velha, the streets are made from sea pebbles – rounded by the waves, carefully selected so that they are all of the same size – which are set in mortar. The cobbles are hardwearing and quickly drain the water away when it rains.

Funchal's main square, the Praça do Município, is elegantly covered in a repeated series of fan shapes, alternately laid in dove-grey basalt and white marble. In modern times the art of making mosaic pavements is not dead: recently completed examples include the Madeiran coat of arms in Praça de Cristovão Colombo, south of the cathedral, and the caravel, compass, sedan chair and wine-carrier with his yoke in Rua João Tavira, northwest of the cathedral.

Decorated paving in Rua João Tavira

Walk: Between the rivers

The first part of this walk is for serious shoppers – there are lots of curious and interesting shops to dip into, from shops selling jewellery next door to shops selling tap washers or salted cod. The walk then explores the area that lies between two of Funchal's rivers – both canalised as a precaution against autumn rains which can see them rise from a trickle to 4m (13ft) in depth.

Allow 30 minutes.

Start in the street that runs northeast of Funchal's cathedral, the Rua do Aljube.

1 Rua do Aljube

There is a good view up this broad street of the cathedral tower with its tile-covered spire, echoed by the tower of the Banco da Madeira, further up. On the left-hand side of the street, Teixeiras (No 15) sells fine embroidered blouses in modern styles and Maison Blanche (No 19) is an upmarket department store. Further up on the right are the stalls of costumed flower sellers under bright umbrellas, and the street widens to form an attractive square. Here you will find the **Bazar do Povo** (Paupers' Bazaar), founded in 1883, a covered shopping mall where numerous retailers on three floors sell everything from table linen and carpets to religious statuary. This lines the whole north side of Rua do Betencourt, which leads to the bridge crossing Ribeira de Santa Luzia. The retaining walls you now see were built

to contain this and the city's other two rivers.

Cross the river to busy Largo do Phelps. Shoppers may want to explore Rua Dr Fernão Ornelas, to the right, which also has interesting shops. Otherwise bear left to Carmo church.

2 Igreja do Carmo

If you are lucky you may find the Carmelite Church open. Inside this 17th-century church, near the high altar, are two very aristocratic tombs shaped like coffins resting on the backs of lions, and *azulejos* (blue and white tiles) depicting scenes from the life of Christ.

Retrace your steps up Rua do Carmo and turn right into Rua Conceição.

3 Rua Conceição

This narrow lane has some of Funchal's oldest buildings, some in a poor state. No 27, for example, is a fine Manueline building beneath the peeling façade, 17th century in date and well worth restoring. Already restored are Nos 49–53 with an ornate balcony, central tower and deep roof eaves. Further up at No 71 you may be lucky to see the blacksmith at work in his forge. Rua Conceição continues on the other side of Rua do Bom Jesus; it is worth continuing up a short way, if only to see No 82, on the right, an embroidery warehouse with tiled façade, cast-iron balconies and an art deco door made for a giant!

Back on Rua do Bom Jesus turn right (west) past the 17th-century Bom Jesus church and cross the river again. As you do so, look right to see the former residence of Henry Veitch, who was British Consul from 1809 to 1836. Veitch designed the towered house himself and it is now occupied by the Instituto do Vinho (Madeira Wine Institute).

4 Praça do Município

On the other side of the river you will pass the rather ugly Palácio da Justiça (Law Courts) on the right with a statue of Justice in front, and then the more attractive main square, the Praça do Município. To the east is the Câmara Municipal, to the south the Bishop's Palace containing the Museu de Arte Sacra (*see pp48–9*), and to the north, with its façade covered in ecstatic saints, is the Jesuit Colégio Church (*see p46*). To the west is the Bar O Leque, a good spot for coffee, shaded by a huge cucumber tree (*Kigelia africana*).

Once refreshed you might like to continue on to the Elegant mansions *walk detailed on pp56–7.*

as you enter you will be greeted by the delicious smell of old wood and wine. The timber buildings surround a cobbled courtyard overlooked by a wisteria-clad balcony. Some of the buildings date back to the 16th century and were part of the island's Franciscan friary which closed in 1834 following the dissolution of all monastic orders operating in Portugal.

Standing in various rooms in the lodge are huge barrels of mahogany and American oak; some 400,000 litres (88,000 gallons) of precious wine are stored here, but this is a small fraction of the 1 million litres (220,000 gallons) a year produced by the Madeira Wine Company alone and of the 4.5 million litres (990,000 gallons) produced by the seven wine companies on the island.

The sheer weight of these storage barrels means that the floors of the

Some very precious bottles of *verdelho* Madeira

wine lodge have to be very strong – hence the massive timbers used as joists and supports are said to have come from ships either wrecked on Madeira or dismantled for salvage once they were no longer seaworthy.

Guided tours

If you join one of the excellent hour-long guided tours offered by the wine lodge you will first be shown an audiovisual presentation detailing the history of Madeira wine. Next you will visit the coopers' yard to watch wine barrels made of oak being repaired, cleaned or marked with branding irons. You will then be taken to the warming rooms where the wine is heated in vast vats for six months using the natural warmth of the sun, assisted by hot-water pipes. Heating is essential to the character of Madeira wine, though its effects were discovered accidentally.

The original Madeira, known as *malmsey*, was a pretty ordinary wine which sailors drank because it was cheap. Barrels of *malmsey* served the double duty of providing ballast and alcoholic stimulation on long sea journeys. Sailors then discovered that the wine improved when it was taken to the tropics, spending weeks or months in a hot hold. Now the wine does not leave Madeira until it has been bottled, but until the end of the 19th century it was still sent on board ship to the equator and back as an essential part of the production process. The other key ingredient is brandy, added to stop the

Museum piece: an ancient wooden wine press

fermentation and fortify the wine, after which the slow process of maturation begins.

As the tour reaches its conclusion you will be taken round a small museum full of leather-bound ledgers, ancient wine presses and old tools, before returning to the downstairs wine bar for a free tasting. After a glass or two of delicious wine you may be tempted to make a purchase, but don't get carried away – some of the rare bottles on offer cost over €250!
Avenida Arriaga 28. Tel: (291) 740110. Open: Mon–Fri 9.30am–6pm, Sat 10am–1pm. Guided tours: Mon–Fri at 10.30, 14.30, 15.30 & 16.30, Sat 11am. Admission charge for the guided tours.

Alfândega Velha

The Alfândega Velha (Old Customs House) is one of Madeira's most ancient buildings, begun around 1477. In the 1970s it was converted to form the home of Madeira's regional parliament. For this reason it is open to the public only on rare occasions (if it is open, do go in to see the fine wood carved ceiling), but you can walk around the exterior to look at the Manueline-style decoration of the stone-carved portals.

The harbourside façade is now hidden by the modern circular debating chamber clad in white marble and widely held to be a blot on the face of a dignified building.
Rua da Alfândega. Not normally open.

Madeira wine

There are four basic types of Madeira, each named after the variety of grape from which they are principally made. *Sercial* is an amber-coloured dry wine, often served as an aperitif or with soup or fish. It is made from grapes grown at around 800m (2,600ft); grapes grown at lower levels increase in sweetness because more of their sugars are concentrated by the sun. Thus, *verdelho*, grown at around 500m (1,640ft), is a medium dry, tawny-coloured wine taken with the main course. The nutty rich *bual* goes well with Stilton or chocolate, while the sweetest Madeira is the rich, dark, mellow *malmsey*, good with after-dinner coffee.

The gradual heating and cooling of the wine and the fortification with cane spirit (a type of brandy) gives Madeira its extraordinary longevity. A reserve wine will already be 5 to 20 years old and vintage Madeira must have spent 20 years in the cask and 2 in the bottle, but these are relative youngsters.

The oldest-surviving bottle dates to 1772 – when the cork was last replaced in 1991 the wine inside was analysed and found to be perfect. You can find wines for sale on Madeira at around €300 that were bottled in 1863, while the American Civil War was still in progress.

Winston Churchill, a regular visitor to Madeira, was fond of the island's noble wines and pointed out that history was being sipped with every glass. At a dinner held at Reid's Hotel in 1950, the British community in Madeira presented Churchill with a bottle that had previously been given to Napoleon when he anchored off the island on the way to exile in St Helena, but the full bottle was

Barrels of maturing wine

never drunk and came back to Madeira. Opening it and sharing it with his fellow guests, Churchill was impressed not so much by the Napoleon connection as by the thought that 'this wine was made when Marie Antoinette was still alive!'

A vintage *bual* Madeira

Avenida do Infante

Art deco villas line your left; on the right is the Savoy Hotel and then the modern Casino Park Hotel. The circular casino in the grounds, shaped like a crown, was designed in the 1970s by Oscar Niemeyer, best known for his work in the Brazilian capital, Brasília. Next on the right is a mansion painted a bougainvillaea pink and protected by an armed guard: this is the **Quinta Vigia**, official residence of Madeira's president.

Avenida do Mar

Those who like boats and marine life will enjoy watching the waterside activities in Funchal's harbour – with luck, a huge ocean-going cruise liner will be in port, or a tall-masted sailing ship. You will also see cargo being unloaded from container ships and boats being repaired. Further along Avenida do Mar is the yacht marina, lined by good seafood restaurants on the landward side. Just before you reach the floating restaurant, turn right and walk out along the sea wall surrounding the marina. This is worth doing for the view as you look back at the island, and for the colourful graffiti painted on the walls by the many people who have sailed to Madeira in yachts from America or Europe.

Casa do Turista

The Casa do Turista, or, as it styles itself, 'The Famous Shop', is more like a museum than a shop, an elegantly furnished town house where all sorts of tempting displays of embroidery and tableware are laid out beneath ornately plastered ceilings.
Rua do Conselheiro José Silvestre Ribeiro 2.

Convento de Santa Clara

The Convent of the Order of Poor Clares was founded in the 15th century by two granddaughters of the island's discoverer, João Gonçalves Zarco. Zarco himself, having lived to the ripe old age of 80, was buried beneath the high altar of the conventual church. His simple tomb slab is not visible, and an imposing 15th-century tomb at the rear of this church is often mistaken for Zarco's; in reality it belongs to his son-in-law, Martim Mendes de Vasconcelos.

Much of the rest of the church was rebuilt in the 17th century and the walls are lined from floor to ceiling with a carpet-like tapestry of yellow, white and blue *azulejos*, making a rich geometric pattern. The timbered ceiling features a painted ship in full sail, as well as floral and heraldic motifs.

The heavy iron grille at the back of the church has an interesting story. Behind it is a stout wooden door which would be opened so that visitors could have limited communication with the nuns who lived in the convent beyond.

It is a reminder of the very isolated and withdrawn lives led by nuns who could not leave their cloistered confinement – though the nuns of this convent did once flee their home in 1566, to escape a piratical attack, journeying inland to the hidden valley now named Curral das Freiras (Nuns' Refuge) in their honour (*see pp100–101*).

The tragic story of Maria Clementina

Many of the nuns were condemned to a life within convent walls by pious or penurious parents, and the case of one such nun became a *cause célèbre* in the 19th century: many foreign visitors to Funchal went to the convent to visit her, providing what little companionship and comfort was possible talking through a metal grille.

Maria Clementina was widely held to be the most beautiful girl on Madeira but her parents forced her to take the veil on her 18th birthday because they were unable to afford the dowry, without which aristocratic young ladies found it hard to find a husband of similar rank. (Placing your daughter in a nunnery was also supposed to confer spiritual benefits on parents and child alike.)

A year later, the newly established liberal government in Lisbon ordered the religious houses to liberate any (*Cont. on p42*)

Santa Clara's tranquil convent cloister, built soon after the island's discovery

Walk: The Old Town

Funchal's Zona Velha (Old Town) is a delightful area of the city where the tastes of well-heeled tourists are catered for in restaurants and nightclubs side by side with some of the poorest slums in the city. The area still has a gritty character but is being redeveloped in places.

Allow 30 minutes.

Start at the Praça da Autonomia.

1 Praça da Autonomia

In the middle of the roundabout is the Autonomy Monument, celebrating the self-governing status Madeira achieved after the 1974 Carnation Revolution. The monument consists of a woman bursting forcefully out of her imprisonment in a block of bronze. This also marks the point where two of Funchal's canalised rivers meet and flow into the sea.

To reach the Old Town proper, walk along the sea walls. After the bus station on your left is a small park and the modern lower station of the cable car to Monte. Leave the sea wall and cross the park to the café-lined Rua Dom Carlos I.

2 Largo do Corpo Santo

This narrow cobbled square gives you a good sense of the Zona Velha's contrasts. Cheek by jowl with numerous pavement cafés specialising in seafood is the shipyard, on the right, belonging to the Madeira Engineering Company, where fishermen's trawlers are repaired. At the far end of the square is the little Capela do Corpo Santo, a simple chapel built by Funchal's fishermen in the 16th century. Beyond the chapel is the Fortaleza de São Tiago, built in 1614 as part of the city's defences. This is now the home of the Museum of Contemporary Art, with works donated by the artists. To the right of the fort, an alley leads through a small shanty town of shacks selling grilled fish to locals who come here to swim from the tiny pebbled Praia da Barreirinha.

Turn left by the fort up Rampa do Forte, then right to reach the church of Santa Maria Maior.

3 Igreja de Santa Maria Maior

This church is situated in the poorest part of Funchal, but the area has benefited from the opening of the Lido swimming complex. The Lido district now has banks, hotels, bars and restaurants. Santa Maria Maior church, opposite the Lido, is also known as the Igreja do Socorro (Church of Salvation) because there is a shrine inside to Apostle St James the Less, who is believed to have helped end a plague that hit the area in the 16th century. The present church is 18th century and has a theatrical air, with its painted ceiling and glass chandeliers, and its gilded pulpit looking like an opera box.

There are excellent views of the sea and of Funchal from the terrace in front of the church.

Turn right out of the church and follow Rua de Santa Maria all the way downhill.

4 Rua de Santa Maria

This street will take you past Arsenio's Fado Restaurant, a popular nightspot where you can hear typical Portuguese *fado* music and song. As you approach the end of the road nearest to the Mercado dos Lavradores, or Workers' Market (*see pp47–8*), you will encounter all the bustle of shoppers, makeshift street stalls and hawkers selling everything from lottery tickets to bunches of garlic and herbs.

Turn right up busy Rua da Boa Viagem and you will soon arrive at the back entrance of the market where fishermen sell their catch. You can also turn left into Rua Latino Coelho and walk round to the front entrance.

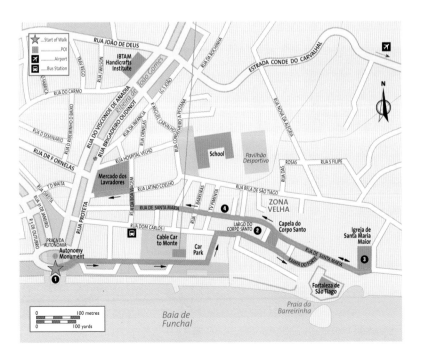

inmates who had been forced into taking monastic vows and who wished to leave. Maria was released, and fell passionately in love with a handsome army officer. Before they could marry, however, Portugal's absolutist monarch dissolved the parliament and revoked all its laws. Maria was forced to return to the convent for the rest of her life.

Abuses such as this eventually led the Portuguese parliament to dissolve all religious establishments, though today the Poor Clares have returned to Santa Clara, where they run a highly regarded school, part of which you will see if you wander through the convent to find the lovely, peaceful 15th-century cloister, planted with citrus trees, which lies to the south of the church.

Calçada Santa Clara.
Open: Mon–Sat 10am–noon & 3–5pm, except public holidays.
If the church door is closed, ring the bell at the convent entrance to the right of the church for admission.

The English Church and British Cemetery

Madeira's English Church is a circular, domed building in neoclassical style which opened in 1822. The architect was Madeira's British Consul, Henry Veitch, who had to work within the constraints of Catholic Portuguese law. This reluctantly allowed the Protestant community on Madeira to build a place of worship, so long as it did not look like a church. The galleried interior is light and airy, lit by fan-shaped windows

The English Church is unrecognisable from the outside as a place of worship

around the base of the dome, and brightened by fine flower arrangements. Surrounding the church is a well-tended garden containing a bust of Philippa of Lancaster, daughter of John of Gaunt and mother of Prince Henry the Navigator. Her marriage to King João I of Portugal in 1387 established the long-standing Portuguese–English alliance. Attached to the nearby chaplaincy is a library containing some 2,500 volumes in English.

The **British Cemetery** is a short walk away, a beautiful and poignant spot full of flowers, lizards, birds and butterflies. Opened in 1887, it contains moving memorials to Protestants of all nations, not just the British. Many record the short lives of hopeful visitors who came to Madeira in search of relief from consumptive diseases but did not long survive. You can also read memorials to several of the German, Polish, Danish and American physicians who came here to treat them.

The English Church, Rua do Quebra Costas 18. Open: daily 9am–5.30pm. Services: see p185.

The British Cemetery, Rua da Carreira 235. Open: daily during daylight hours (ring the bell at the gate for entry).

Hospício da Princesa

Very few visitors ever find their way into the well-tended gardens of this hospital, though they are open to the public. The hospital itself dates from 1859 when it was founded as a sanatorium for tuberculosis sufferers by Doña Amelia, wife of Emperor Pedro I of Brazil, as a memorial to their daughter, who died from the disease.

IBTAM Handicrafts Institute

Crafts are such an important part of the Madeiran economy that this institute was set up to provide training and monitor standards. It is principally concerned with the arts of embroidery, tapestry and wickerwork. A small museum on the first floor of the institute's headquarters building displays some very fine examples of all three.

Climbing the stairs to the museum you will be greeted by a massive tapestry *The Allegory of Madeira*, designed by Gino Ramoli and made between 1958 and 1961. The tapestry, depicting a typically flower-filled Madeiran landscape, contains a total of 7 million stitches, the work of 14 girls.

The museum itself consists of cases full of embroidered tablecloths, bedspreads and diaphanous nightgowns, all of which will appeal to connoisseurs of fine needlework.

Also on display are some interesting examples of island costume, including colourful hand-embroidered waistcoats, blouses and scarves, and a small exhibition showing how embroidery designs are transferred, using inked rollers, to the fabric before the embroiderers begin their work.

Rua do Visconde de Anadia 44. Tel: (291) 223141. Open: Mon–Fri 10am–12.30pm & 2.30–5.30pm. Admission charge.

Town houses

Central Funchal has many fine town houses, most of them built during the 19th century. The grandest are known as *quintas*, roughly translated as 'mansion' or 'manor house'. Rural *quintas* are usually set in extensive grounds and are connected with some form of agriculture, such as wine production. In the town, *quinta* was simply the name given to the residence of a wealthy or prominent citizen. The dominant architectural style is baroque, but in Madeira there is a very restrained version of this often theatrical style. Door and window surrounds are usually carved into curvaceous shapes but the black-grey basalt used as building stone is too hard for elaborate moulding. Instead, the city's architects achieved their impact through colour, contrasting the soft black of the window and door frames with the gleaming white of the rendered walls into which they are set. Wrought-iron balconies running the full length of the house ornament smaller houses, many of which are built around a plant-filled patio. Balconies, window shutters, gates and doors are traditionally painted green and the roofs covered in terracotta tiles, so that looking down on the city from above, or approaching by ship, you will see landmark buildings, such as the cathedral tower, pointing a white finger above a sea of warm red. Legislation was passed in 1986 requiring owners to stick to these time-honoured colours, hence the pleasing harmony of the buildings in central Funchal.

Plants and the play of sunlight and shadow add to the delightful variety of Funchal's architecture

Delicate patterns wrought from iron

Igreja do Colégio

The baroque façade of this collegiate church dominates Funchal's main square, though it is not the most attractive on Madeira, and the gesticulating Jesuit saints filling the niches look in danger of toppling over in their frenzy of religious ecstasy.

The interior is more likeable, with its geometric *azulejos* and its altar surrounds, carved in gilded wood and plaster, featuring fat pink cherubs climbing through a tangle of vine leaves. The decoration mostly dates from the period 1641 to 1660, although the church itself was founded in 1574, soon after the Jesuits were granted permission to establish a seminary here.

After the Jesuits were expelled from Portugal in 1759, the college was turned into a military barracks. It has now been designated part of the campus of Madeira's nascent university.

Praça do Município. Open: daily 5–6pm & for services.

The façade of the Jesuit church fronting Funchal's main square

Produce to tempt all the senses on sale in the bustling Workers' Market

Jardim de São Francisco

This most central of Funchal's public gardens offers a shady retreat close to the Tourist Information Office and is a popular place where Madeirans, young and old, meet to gossip and pass the time of day. It also contains some magnificent trees (most of which are labelled) planted in the 19th century, when Franciscan monks, along with all religious orders, were expelled from Portugal.

This garden was created for public use on the site of their ruined friary, and amid the lush foliage you can still see the stone-carved coat of arms which once decorated the friary gateway.

Avenida Arriaga. Open: 24 hours.

Mercado dos Lavradores

The Workers' Market is one of the most compelling and colourful sights on Madeira, a bustling place which touches on all aspects of island life, not just food. Friday is the best day to visit it because peasant farmers from all over the island arrive in the market on that day, bringing their produce for sale. Makeshift stalls are set up in the streets and in the car park to the south of Rua Dom Carlos I.

Even if you do not want to shop, the market is worth visiting for the magnificent displays, especially those of the costumed flower sellers at the entrance to the covered market, and those of the fruit and vegetable vendors on the ground floor. Those who are squeamish about seeing fish being gutted and filleted should, perhaps, give the basement fish market a miss.

The prices, both for fruit and for fish, are relatively low, and you will soon realise why most of the island's farmers have to survive on a very meagre income. Even so, most market traders usually find a few euros to spare when the lottery ticket sellers do their rounds of the market, offering the chance to buy that dream ticket to end all financial worries.

Rua Dr Fernão Ornelas. Open: Mon–Fri 7am–8pm, Sat 7am–2pm.

Monumento a João Gonçalves Zarco

Just beyond the palace, the statue of Zarco, the island's discoverer, was carved by Madeiran sculptor Francisco Franco (*see pp49–50*) and unveiled in 1934. On the northwestern corner of the square is the splendid **Banco de Portugal** building, with decorative swags, baskets of fruit and human

João Gonçalves Zarco, who discovered the Madeira islands, is commemorated in Funchal

figures carved in marble and grey basalt contrasting with gleaming white walls.

Across Avenida Zarco is the regional government building with its huge tiled entrance, while the next building, the **Banco Nacional Ultramarino**, has a pretty art deco lamp on its entrance stairs.

Museu de Arte Sacra

This museum will delight the art connoisseur in you. Housed in an 18th-century building that was once the Episcopal Court is a priceless collection of Renaissance Flemish paintings, considered to be the best in Portugal.

In the 15th and 16th centuries Portugal's trade with Flanders was very strong, creating a market for Flemish art. Government and church officials, along with plantation owners, were anxious to decorate their churches and residences with these spiritual works of art.

Opened in 1955, the museum was created specifically for these paintings, many of which had been left neglected for years in residences and churches all over the island. An ambitious restoration programme by the Museu de Arte Antiga in Lisbon, the country's foremost restoration museum, was started in the 1930s to save these master paintings from virtual rack and ruin.

The Flemish collection, displayed on the top floor, has works such as *Descending from the Cross* by Gerard

David (1460–1523), *The Annunciation* by Joos Van Cleve (1508–45) and the *Triptych of St James the Less and St Philip* by Pieter Coecke Van Aelst (*c.*1502–50). Also on display is a very moving 16th-century oak sculpture of Christ from the Flemish school and a Marinus Van Reymerswaele 16th-century portrait of St Jerome.

The middle floor of the museum has displays of clerical garments, delicately embroidered vestments and church silver. Definitely not as interesting as the Flemish art, but worth a look.
Rua do Bispo 21. Tel: (291) 228900. Open: Tue–Sat 10am–12.30pm & 2.30–6pm, Sun 10am–1pm. Admission charge.

Museu Cidade do Açúcar (Sugar Museum)

Formerly housed in the Town Hall, this museum, located north of the beautiful Praça de Colombo, has seen the number of its exhibits documenting Madeira's sugar trade drastically reduced. The museum now occupies the building that was the home of João Esmeraldo, a 14th-century sugar merchant.

Locally the house is known as 'Columbus's House' because reportedly Christopher Columbus was a guest of the Esmeraldo family in 1498.

The original house was demolished in 1876. During excavation in 1986 several important archaeological finds were revealed, including the house's original well, given a place of honour in the museum. Sadly, most of the exhibits and the timeline of Madeira's history that decorated the walls of the Town Hall are not in the new museum. What is on display are a few sugar moulds dating from the 15th century and some 16th-century ceramics and religious icons.

The museum is not something to go out of your way for; stop in if you are at the Praça de Colombo.
Praça de Colombo 5. Open: Mon–Fri 10am–12.30pm & 2–6pm. Admission charge.

Museu Franco

Art lovers should make the effort to see this excellent but quiet museum displaying the work of the two Franco de Sousa brothers. Henrique (1883–1961) was a painter and Francisco (1885–1955) was a sculptor. Though born on Madeira, both spent much of their lives working in Lisbon and in Paris, where they were much influenced by the artistic milieux of Picasso, Degas and Modigliani.

Henrique experimented with various styles, so there are numerous canvases displayed here that will remind you of Van Gogh, Gauguin and Cézanne, but he eventually found his forte as a portrait painter; his pictures are fresh, colourful and airy, and he endows all his sitters with character and nobility, be they peasants with fascinating, weatherworn faces or pampered aristocrats seated in their gardens.

Francisco is the better known of the two brothers simply because his statues, such as the Zarco monument marking the centre of Funchal, and the *Semeador* (Sower) in the Parque de Santa Catarina (*see pp58–9*), are familiar city landmarks. The displays covering his work include a number of commemorative statues, working drawings and lithographs, as well as his designs for medals, coins and postage stamps.

Rua João de Deus 13. Tel: (291) 230633. Open: daily 10am–12.30pm & 2–6pm. Free admission.

Museu Frederico de Freitas

This absorbing museum is in two parts. The first consists of hundreds of cartoons, engravings and paintings of Madeira, most of them dating from the 19th century, hung round the walls of a two-storey gallery. The eyes glaze over after a while faced with such a mass of material, much of which derives from the hands of amateur artists.

Even so, it is interesting to see how these artists have responded to the island's dramatic landscapes, so different in their elemental force from the gentle pastoral scenes that the artists were trained to draw. There is also an amusing sequence of pictures by Isabella de França from the journal she kept on her visit to Portugal and Madeira in 1853–4. Isabella was honest enough to admit her paintings were a bit crude, but they do record what she experienced with frankness and humour.

All these pictures were bequeathed to Madeira in 1978 by the lawyer Dr Frederico de Freitas, along with his house, which forms the second part of the museum. This charming old residence was built in the late 17th century by the Counts of Calçada, but with splendid art nouveau additions, including the little *salon vitré* (conservatory) in the garden designed for sitting in and admiring the views, and the wonderful, intimate Winter Garden, with its cane furniture, doors and hanging lamp, all in the art nouveau style. The stately rooms are crammed with objects collected by Dr de Freitas, from fine furniture, carpets and religious paintings to an extraordinary collection of some 2,000 jugs.

There is also an important collection of hand-painted *azulejos*, but the most endearing items are the crib figures and Madonnas carved in wood in the 17th and 18th centuries, some from the distant outposts of the Portuguese empire, such as Goa and Macao.

Calçada Santa Clara 7. Tel: (291) 220578. Open: Tue–Sat 10am–5.30pm. Admission charge.

Museu Municipal

The Municipal Museum is much more fun than the rather bureaucratic name suggests. Downstairs there is an aquarium and also displays of stuffed sharks, as well as birds, mammals and other forms of Madeiran wildlife. Older children will enjoy staring into the gaping jaws of the sharks and imagining what it might be like to be

The inviting art nouveau interior of the Freitas Winter Garden

munched by those terrifying, razor-sharp teeth. There are plenty of uglier specimens to feed your nightmares, including bloated prickly porcupine fish and a giant crab with claws almost a metre long. Some of the displays are very realistic. The island's birds, for instance, are shown as if feeding their young in the nest, surrounded by all the debris and droppings you would expect. The aquarium below is pitch dark except for the large tanks containing typical Madeiran fish and marine vegetation: try spotting the flounders, masters of camouflage; wonder at the beauty of the sea anemones; see how crabs walk underwater – balletically, on the tips of their claws – watched by brooding surly lobsters and weird beasts such as the scorpion fish. Altogether this museum is a good introduction to the island's wildlife as well as being an enjoyable place to pass a rainy hour or so.

Rua da Mouraria 31. Tel: (291) 229761.
Open: Tue–Fri 10am–6pm, Sat–Sun &
public holidays noon–6pm.
Admission charge.

Island costume

The flower sellers of Funchal's Mercado dos Lavradores (*see pp47–8*) all wear the distinctive costume of the island. For women this means a striped woollen skirt worn with a red embroidered waistcoat, beautiful pleated blouse, and a shoulder scarf.

Red is the dominant colour, but the scarlet stripes of the skirt alternate with yellow, black, green, blue or white stripes – the precise colour combinations differ from one village to another, as do the embroidery patterns on the scarf and waistcoat.

Folk dancers in traditional costumes

Soft, supple boots enable Madeirans to walk long distances

Similarly, the colours in the waist sash worn by the men provide a clue to their home village. The sash is worn with a white linen shirt and baggy, knee-length trousers. You will often see men wearing bobble hats as you tour the island, knitted with ear flaps as a precaution against the cold winds that can blow above 800m (2,600ft). For special occasions both men and women wear the *carapuça*, a small black or blue skull cap with a long tassel. Both sexes also wear boots called *botachas*. These are made of naturally tanned cowhide and goatskin, with the upper part turned down to the ankles and trimmed with a red band. Madeiran song and folk dance groups, who regularly perform in Funchal's hotels and restaurants, take their art very seriously and aim to keep island customs alive – they will show you and explain different parts of their costume. There is a small display of authentic historical costume, showing regional variations, in the IBTAM museum (see p43).

Angel's trumpet flowers in the lush gardens of the Museu Quinta das Cruzes

Museu Quinta das Cruzes

The Quinta das Cruzes (literally 'The Mansion of the Crosses') is an elegant and airy house which gives a taste of the lifestyle once enjoyed by Madeira's most wealthy inhabitants. It is said that Grande Capitão Zarco, Madeira's discoverer and Funchal's first ruler, had his house on this site, splendidly situated high on a hill above the city.

Now the house is surrounded by suburbs, though the world is kept at bay by the high garden wall and the extensive gardens, which have been designated as an 'archaeological park' where 15th- and 16th-century tombstones, coats of arms, and architectural mouldings are displayed among the lush vegetation.

The two most striking exhibits are the huge stone window frames set on the lawn to the left of the museum entrance, carved with little man-eating lions, dancing figures and rope motifs. Some would have you believe that these come from the house in which Christopher Columbus lived on Madeira (*see p17*); in fact they date from 1517 and are a fine example of the ornate Manueline style, which flourished during the reign of Manuel I of Portugal (1490–1520). In the rest of the garden you will find frog-filled ponds, dragon trees (*Dracaena draco*) with claw-like aerial roots and bark like the skin of a reptile, and a big display of pot-grown orchids (in flower from late November to early April).

The present house dates largely from the early 19th century when the original 17th-century structure was rebuilt by the Lomelino family, wealthy Genoese wine shippers who furnished it in the typical style of the period. There are many delicate pieces of furniture in the Regency Trafalgar style, made from the local *vinhático* wood (*Persea indica*), similar in colour to mahogany, as well as pieces by Chippendale and Hepplewhite which the owners of the mansion may have purchased from visiting tourists; it was the practice, in the 19th century, for visitors wintering on the island to bring their own furniture and then sell it off at the end of their stay to pay the rent, as well as the servants' wages and the grocer's bills.

Each room of the mansion has a different theme. Room 4 contains art from India and China imported by the Portuguese East India Company, notably a watery-blue silk wall hanging embroidered with butterflies from northern India and a rare Cizhou-ware vase made in China in the 13th century.

European art features in Room 5, including a Flemish painting by Jean de Mabuse of the *Three Magi* (1470). A huge 18th-century Aubusson carpet and a tapestry of similar date, featuring dancing peasants, set the theme for the French style of Room 6. In Room 9, do not miss the big oil painting of Funchal, one of several topographical views set about the house. Room 10 contains 19th-century costumes and jewellery – from full dress uniforms to lace and linen nightclothes. In Room 11, there are tender crib figures of painted clay, made in the 18th and 19th centuries.

Downstairs, in the former kitchens and basements, is a miscellaneous collection, including a series of satirical lithographs poking fun at Madeiran dress and manners, especially those of the clergy, who are portrayed as fat and self-indulgent. Here, too, are finds from the Dutch East India ship the *Slot ter Hooge*, wrecked off Porto Santo in 1724 and salvaged in 1974.

Finally, there are some fine examples of cupboards made out of recycled packing cases – not today's flimsy affairs, but 17th-century versions made of stout hardwoods which, once Madeira's sugar trade died, were taken apart and made into furniture. *Calçada do Pico 1. Museum open: Tue–Sun 10am–12.30pm & 2–5.30pm. Gardens open: Tue–Sun 10am–6pm. Admission charge. Bus: 15a from Praça da Autonomia.*

Palácio de São Lourenço

This palace, built in the 16th century to defend Funchal from pirate attacks, is still the headquarters of Madeira's military command. It houses a small museum.

Walk: Elegant mansions

The main purpose of this route is to track down the best of Madeira's ornate town houses, but with plenty of other distractions along the way.

Allow 30 minutes for the walk – half a day or more if you visit all the churches and museums along the route.

Start in Praça do Município and walk west out of the square, along Rua Câmara Pestana. Cross Avenida Zarco into Rua da Carreira.

1 Rua da Carreira

This is one of Funchal's most interesting streets, lined with ornate buildings. The predominant colours are white, grey and green. Most of the owners keep to this colour scheme, but the effect is far from monotonous because every building is different and some have exuberant displays of plants on their balconies.

The **Museu Photographia Vicentes** (Photography Museum) has recently been restored and it contains around 380,000 negatives and images of life and important events on Madeira. Continuing into the courtyard, there is an open-air shaded café. Worth stopping at further up on the left, at No 75, is a baker's shop, noted for its *bolo de mel*, the so-called honey cake, black and dense with nuts and fruit, but actually made with molasses. No 83 has an ancient shop sign declaring itself to be the *Rei das Mobílias* – King of Furnishings; it sells antique and reproduction furniture. Opposite, No 102 has a good selection of wickerwork, including baskets, chairs and tables.

Take a look up Rua do Sardo, the next right, which has many more ornate houses. No 7, on the left, is one of the most plant-filled balconies on the island, a veritable cascade of ferns, geraniums and jade-green succulents. Back on Rua da Carreira, No 155 (the local army recruiting office), on the left, is one of the best buildings on the street, with long balconies on both upper floors made of wrought iron in a delicate fan-shaped pattern.

At the next right, Rua da Mouraria, look up to see Nos 3–5, their windows gaily garlanded with floral motifs.

At the next right, you can turn up Rua do Quebra Costas to see the English Church at No 18, built in the early 19th century, and set in a pretty garden (*see pp42–3*).

Continuing up Rua da Carreira you will finally reach the iron gates of the British Cemetery (ring for entry) with its moving memorials set in a tranquil bird-filled garden (see p43). Coming out of the cemetery, turn left, then right into Rua das Cruzes.

2 Rua das Cruzes

Towering above you is the **Castelo de São João do Pico**, the Peak Fort, built between 1580 and 1640 when Madeira (as well as all Portugal) was ruled by Spain. The massive fort is now used by the Portuguese Admiralty as a radio station, and so is closed to the public. *Follow Rua das Cruzes round to the right. Bear right where the road divides, then climb the steps to the left and walk up to the terrace shaded by a huge Indian fig tree. From here there are good views over the English Church and out to the sea. Continue on beneath the walls of the Quinta das Cruzes, the lovely 17th-century villa and garden built on the site where Zarco, Madeira's discoverer, had his house (see pp54–5). Turn right here, down Calçada Santa Clara.*

3 Calçada Santa Clara

Santa Clara church (*see p38*) is where Zarco is buried. From here, continue down the steep road past the Museu Frederico de Freitas, another fascinating and elegant house open to the public (*see p50*). At the bottom of the hill you will reach the **Igreja São Pedro**. The main attraction of this church, built in 1598 and remodelled in 1748, is the gilded altar surround and the ceiling painted with flowers, including roses, day lilies, Turk's cap lilies and chrysanthemums. To the right of São Pedro, in Rua da Mouraria, is the Museu Municipal (*see pp50–51*). *Opposite São Pedro, Rua das Pretas will take you back to the starting point of the walk.*

Museu Fortaleza

The Fortress Museum is located within the bastions of the palace and is entered through a splendid 16th-century carved stone portal. The museum traces the history of the fortress from its construction in the 1520s to its later conversion into the official residence of the island's two governors – one military, one civilian. On display are historic guns, cannon, armour and photographs of the palace as it is today, complete with titillating 19th-century ceiling frescoes of Neptune and a retinue of blowsy mermaids.

Photographs are as close as you can get to the main building, which is still the residence of Madeira's armed forces' Commander-in-Chief and guarded by goose-stepping, sword-carrying soldiers.

Avenida Arriaga (opposite the Tourist Information Office). Open: Free tours on *Wed at 9.30am & Fri at 3pm, but you will need to schedule a tour by calling (291) 202530 or visit the main tourist office. The National Palace can be visited only if you have had a previous appointment with the office of the prime minister. Free admission.*

Symbol of Madeira's fertility, Francisco Franco's statue of the *Semeador*, the Sower

Parque de Santa Catarina

If you walk to central Funchal from the Hotel Zone on a regular basis you will soon get to know this public park on the hillside overlooking the harbour. A mini botanical garden, it contains a number of fine specimen trees planted in the late 1940s when the garden was converted from a disused cemetery. Fountains and aviaries dot the park, as do some industrial relics – a steamroller and a sugar-cane mill, for example.

There is also an open-air café and a children's adventure playground. A bronze sculpture of a sower dating from 1919, the work of Francisco Franco (*see pp49–50*), stands on the main lawn of the park, while lower down, near the Capela de Santa Catarina, is a statue of Christopher Columbus and a modernistic fountain featuring a prone female torso.

The chapel itself dates from 1425. It was built on the orders of Zarco's wife, Constança Rodrigues, and is the oldest place of worship on Madeira.

The body of the little chapel has been rebuilt several times – most recently in the 17th century – but the porch still shelters the original holy water stoup, carved with the wheel of St Catherine.

Looking down from the terrace where the chapel sits, you can see the traffic roundabout known as the Rotunda do Infante. Here is a statue of Henry the Navigator seated beneath a rather ugly stone arch and looking across to a fountain of sea horses supporting a globe.

Avenida do Infante. Open: 24 hours.

Quinta da Boa Vista

The Quinta da Boa Vista, sometimes referred to by its old name, the Garton Greenhouses, is well worth visiting if you are interested in plants and gardens. The Quinta specialises in growing orchids for the cut-flower market, propagating the microscopic seeds (each seed head can produce 5 million seeds) and nurturing them through the critical first four years of their life until the tiny plants are ready to be taken out of their test tubes and exposed to the open air. Extraordinarily delicate in the early years, they then become unbelievably tough – surviving, seemingly, in dust-dry soil with no visible means of nutrition. Being epiphytes, they derive their nourishment from moisture in the air, and Madeira's humid climate provides ideal living conditions. Though most orchids flower only in winter (the first blooms appear in late November and the flowering period continues until early April), the lovingly tended gardens around the Quinta da Boa Vista make a visit worthwhile at any time of year. You

Exotics of the plant world: a carefully nurtured orchid at Quinta da Boa Vista

can also buy orchids and flowers to take home (*see pp145–6*).

Rua Lombo da Boa Vista. Tel: (291) 220468. Open: Mon–Sat 9am–5.30pm. Admission charge.

Sé (Cathedral)

Funchal's cathedral was begun in 1485 and completed in 1514. Its construction marked a major stage in Funchal's development. Previously it had been a small frontier town at the edge of the known world, a place full of adventurers, slaves and refugees, beyond the reach of law and religion. Now it was thought worthy of a cathedral and the King of Portugal himself, Manuel I, sent two master-builders to supervise the work, along with the gift of a fine processional cross (now in the Museu de Arte Sacra, see pp48–9).

Naturally, the cathedral was built in the Manueline style, named after the king, a late Gothic development noted for inventive decorations reflecting nautical themes (anchors, ropes, fish) and the kind of strange birds, animals and flowers that Portuguese explorers were beginning to see in newly discovered parts of the world.

The playful Manueline details of Funchal's cathedral are best seen from the streets to the south of the church, looking up to the barley-sugar pinnacles rising from the roof near the tower. Equally exotic are the designs on the nave ceiling, though these are difficult to see in the very dark interior: they are picked out in white ivory against a background of carved wood from the native Madeiran tree, variously known as juniper or prickly cedar (*Juniperus cedrus*). If the cathedral doors are open they may allow in just enough light to let you view the choir stalls, carved out of the same wood and painted blue and gold. The stalls depict saints, apostles and evangelists but in the clothing of the 17th century, when they were carved, and so providing an insight into contemporary (male) fashion. Sadly, even with the doors open you will have to take it on trust that the altar is surrounded by 16th-century Flemish and Portuguese paintings – it really is too dark to see, though you can get an idea of the rich splendour if you come here when the chancel is lit up for a service, or for the occasional classical concerts, which take advantage of the cathedral's fine acoustics.

Rua do Aljube. Open: daily during daylight hours, except for lunch 12.30–2.30pm. Free admission.

Teatro Municipal

The Municipal Theatre was built in 1888 and has boxes rising vertically in tiers, modelled on the Little Theatre at Versailles. Often there is an art exhibition in the foyer, which enables you to go in and look around.

The theatre bar, open to the street with its tree-shaded garden area, is a popular meeting place among bohemian Madeirans.

A typical Madeiran carved and gilded altar frame in Funchal cathedral

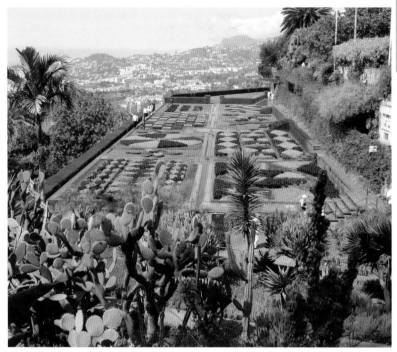

Cacti and palm trees fringe the formal gardens

Next to the theatre is an even more ornate building, now a Toyota showroom, decorated with *azulejos* showing 1920s visitors being carried in a hammock and riding a toboggan from Monte. Opposite is the colourful Jardim de São Francisco (*see p47*), a garden full of tropical trees and shrubs built on the site of the former Franciscan friary.

FUNCHAL ENVIRONS
Jardim Botânico

The whole of Madeira is one vast botanical garden where plants grow in extraordinary profusion, thanks to the combination of fertile volcanic soils, sunshine, regular rainfall and high humidity. The Botanical Garden is the place to learn more about the island's exotic flora and enjoy the magnificent setting and the views.

The Botanical Garden first opened to the public in 1960. Before that it was a private estate appropriately called the Quinta do Bom Sucesso (Good Fortune Estate) belonging to the Reid family, founders of Reid's Hotel (*see pp174–5*).

The Reids' former residence now houses a Natural History Museum (*Cont. on p64*)

Flowers

Madeira's roadside verges, *levada* paths and public parks are bright with flowers throughout the year. Thanks to the introduction of many South African plants which bloom in the depths of the northern hemisphere's winter, the botanical interest can be just as great in December as in August, and visitors arriving for Christmas festivities are greeted by rampant red agave flowers lining the airport road into Funchal. Some flowers bloom all year in Madeira's equable climate, including oleanders, red- and orange-flowered hibiscus and the aptly named Bird of Paradise (*Strelitzia reginae*) with its pointed, crest-like inflorescences. Winter-

The tropical orchid, a native of South Africa

Indian fig tree and Mediterranean hibiscus

flowering plants include poinsettias, introduced from South America, with their scarlet leaves and gold stamens, camellias, orchids and arum lilies.

The many different varieties of mimosa that grow in the island's woods are also covered in powder-puff yellow flowers at this time of year. This woodland display is bettered only by the flowering of the jacaranda trees in central Funchal in April and May. Planted along all Funchal's main roads, their massed blossoms form a river of lilac blue when viewed from above – descending from the hotel district, for example. Even as the jacaranda

blossoms drop, the Pride of Bolivia (*Tipuana tipu*) picks up the baton, flowering in Avenida Zarco from June through much of the summer.

Summer is the season of massed agapanthus, which grow wild along the waysides, of fragrant giant honeysuckles, of the even sweeter frangipani, and literally hundreds of other plants. Some will seem familiar, most of them wonderfully exotic.

If you want a basic illustrated guide, *The Plants and Flowers of Madeira* by António da Costa and Luis de O Franquinho is good value for money and widely available on the island.

located just inside the entrance gates. This contains cases full of fossils, fish, insects and stuffed birds – all of which look rather dusty with age and far from lifelike. There are, however, one or two more impressive exhibits, such as the massive piece of fossilised tree heather (*Erica scoparia*) which would have grown to an even greater girth had its life not been ended by volcanic eruptions 10 million years ago.

Immediately around the museum is an area devoted to orchids (in flower from November to April). Another area is planted with species indigenous to Madeira – plants which are not found anywhere else in the world in the wild. Some of these have, of course, been disseminated by botanists and horticulturalists to other parts of the world since their original discovery, including the Madeiran cranesbill (*Geranium maderense*) with its handsome ferny foliage and masses of magenta flowers.

Paths radiate from the museum to various points of the garden. If you want to explore the site systematically, climb to the top of the garden first, to the so-called Lovers' Grotto and viewpoint.

From this high point, a series of terraces descends down the hillside to an open-air café, set amid carp-filled ponds, and rampant stands of papyrus grass. The lower terraces are more regimented than the woodland areas higher up – indeed, one area is devoted to commercial plants grown for the cut-flower trade and as seasonal bedding.

The bedding plants are planted in geometric patterns designed to show off their foliage colours, ranging from sulphur yellow to grey and deep purple; one block even spells out *Bemvindo* (welcome) in beetroot red.

After this the sparse simplicity of the cactus and succulent beds comes as something of a relief to the eye. If you are lucky, some of these splendid and massive plants will be in flower, the exotic colours of the blossoms contrasting with the sculptural simplicity of the trunk and branches.

Caminho do Meio, Quinta do Bom Sucesso (3km/1¾ miles from Funchal). www.madeirabotancialgarden.com. Gardens open: daily 9am–6pm. Museum open: daily 9am–12.30pm & 1.30–5.30pm. Admission charge. Bus: 29, 30, 31 or taxi from Funchal, cable car from Monte.

Jardim dos Loiros

While exploring the Jardim Botânico you will hear a constant chorus of hoots, whoops and screeches emanating from the adjacent property. If your curiosity is aroused, you can try to discover the source of all this noise by taking a short downhill walk from the entrance to the Botanical Garden to the Jardim dos Loiros (Tropical Bird Garden). Here, amid well-tended gardens, are the noise-makers: some birds flying freely where they want, and

A mass of agapanthus at the Jardim Botânico

others within the aviaries dotting the grounds. The various cockatoos, parrots and parakeets are as gaudily coloured as the flowers and some reveal even more striking colours when they open their wings to fly. You will enjoy the sight of these colourful birds so long as your conscience is not troubled by the knowledge that they are kept in such an unstimulating environment. A bare concrete cage is a long way from the South American jungle.

Caminho do Meio. Open: daily 9am–6pm. Admission charge. Ticket for Jardim Botânico Parque includes entrance to Jardim dos Loiros. Bus: 29, 30, 31 or taxi from Funchal, cable car from Monte.

Jardim Orquídea

This tiny garden, located some 200m (220yds) from the Jardim Botânico

(*see pp61 & 64*), allows you to view the different processes involved in commercial orchid production. During the flowering season (from the end of November to early April), the shade houses and polythene tunnels are full of exotic blooms – some spidery, some fat and waxy, spotted or plain, and in every colour from brown, black and purple to electric blue, yellow and green.

For the rest of the year, unless you are an orchid fanatic, the garden is not one of Madeira's most compelling attractions because there is little to see except for displays covering the propagation and development of orchid seeds.

Rua Pita da Silva 37. Open: daily 10am–5pm. Admission charge. Bus: 29, 30, 31 or taxi from Funchal, cable car from Monte.

Around Funchal

Moving out of the capital, you will discover the exotic gardens and manor houses of the rich, and the fishing villages and tiny farms where the majority of Madeirans eked out a living from the sea or land. Picturesque villages nestle below dramatic towering cliffs where every bit of usable slope has been terraced. Majestic gardens surrounding their quintas are perched on the hillsides to give sweeping views for their owners. Each, though, presents a different facet of Madeiran life and traditions.

Cabo Girão

Cabo Girão is one of the most heavily promoted sights on Madeira, billed as the second-highest sea cliff in Europe and one of the highest in the world. Guides tend to be rather vague if you ask which is Europe's highest cliff. Pedantic questions are silenced by the truly impressive views down an almost sheer drop to the Atlantic, 580m (1,900ft) below. The name of the headland means 'Cape of the Turning', not because the view makes your head spin, but because Zarco sailed this far on his first exploratory trip to Madeira before turning back to Funchal, where he put down his anchor and decided to land. Those who can bear to look down the cliff face for very long will see terraces dug into the cliff face. It scarcely seems credible that anyone would dare cultivate such tiny and vertiginous plots, and yet the warmth of the south-facing cliffs has tempted some brave farmers to plant vines, flowers and vegetables.

On the south coast, 22km (13 2/3 miles) west of Funchal.

Câmara de Lobos

Sir Winston Churchill, the British war-time prime minister, is regarded with almost saintly reverence on Madeira because he helped to put the island on the tourist map. From 1949 he made regular visits to paint the local landscape and, in particular, the little fishing village of Câmara de Lobos. Now a plaque on the wall alongside the busy 101 road east of the harbour marks the spot where Churchill sat to paint the view, and local shops sell rather fuzzy black and white postcards of the great man at work, unmistakable with his trademark cigar and Panama hat. It is interesting to speculate how much the fishing village has changed since Churchill's day. It looks as pretty as ever, with gaily painted boats drawn up on the tiny pebble beach. The tiny harbourside houses are painted in the same bright colours – primary red, yellow, blue and green against brilliant white. Yet there is an air of distressing poverty about the place, with several of the boats pulled up on shore and looking sadly neglected. The fishermen here work all night to catch *espada* (scabbard fish) which are then sold in the harbourside wholesale market. You will have to come very early to see this in operation, since most of the trading is over by 7am.

A tiny chapel in the bar district hints at the hardships of the fishing life:

scenes from the life of St Nicholas, patron saint of seafarers, include vivid depictions of shipwrecks and drownings.

8km (5 miles) west of Funchal.

Monte

For a breathtaking ride to Monte take the cable car from Funchal's Zona Velha (Old Town). You will arrive in Monte at Largo das Barboses where just a short walk will take you to the shorter and more recently built cable car ride to the

Looking up to Cabo Girão

Jardim Botânico, one of several *levada* walks and the sights of Monte.

Monte stands at 550m (1,804ft) above sea level and the steep uphill journey used to be made by rack-and-pinion railway. It opened in 1893 and carried visitors from Funchal up the hillside, past the colourful gardens of numerous rural villas and mansions, to the station at Monte, taking 20 minutes to make the climb. Disaster struck in 1919 when one of the boilers of the steam locomotive exploded, killing four people and injuring many more. From then on, visitors and locals alike turned their back on the railway, regarding it as a dangerous means of transport. The line closed in 1939 but is currently being reinstated.

A short stretch of elevated viaduct survives from the old railway and this is the first sight that greets today's visitors arriving by car or bus. The station building survives on the shady main square, Largo do Fonte. The palatial station building, which opened in 1912, also served as a restaurant. Today it continues to be used for receptions and functions. Passengers visiting Madeira on luxury cruise liners are often brought here for cocktails and to enjoy the expansive views down over the grey-green heads of fragrant eucalyptus trees to the red roofs of Funchal below.

The station garden, first laid out in 1894, has the rather formal outlines that have now been softened by the rampant green creepers that have cloaked the railway bridge in green and pushed out tendrils to spiral up the trunks of the tree ferns, obviously thriving in Monte's humid climate.

An extreme and thrilling way to descend back to Funchal is via the historic toboggan ride (*see p73*); white-suited drivers wait for passengers at the foot of the steps leading to the Monte church.

Monte Palace Tropical Gardens

A short stroll from the cable car brings you to this garden; one that promises to be the best on Madeira as it approaches full maturity. The 7ha (17 acres) of hillside surrounding Monte Palace have been skilfully planted with areas devoted to Madeiran flora, oriental species, azaleas, ferns and orchids. *Caminho do Monte 174. Tel: (291) 742650. www.montepalace.com. Open: daily 9.30am–6.00pm. Admission charge.*

Nossa Senhora do Monte (Our Lady of Monte)

The twin-towered church of Nossa Senhora do Monte is a prominent landmark high on the hillside above Funchal. To devout Madeiran Catholics, the church is a constant reminder of the Virgin Mary's protective role as the island's patron saint.

Pilgrims who visit Monte will climb the 74 steep steps of the church on their knees. The handsome church stands on the site of a chapel built in 1470 by Adam Gonçalves Ferreira. He and his twin sister Eve were the first children born on Madeira. The church was rebuilt in baroque style following an earthquake, and re-dedicated in 1818. Inside, in a silver tabernacle above the altar, is a precious statue of the Virgin which is carried in procession on the Feast of the Assumption. More imposing is the black coffin chest in the chapel to the left (north) of the nave which contains the mortal remains of the Emperor Charles I, the last in the long line of Habsburg emperors.

(*Cont. on p72*)

Discussing the catch at the fishing village of Câmara de Lobos

The grape harvest

The grape harvest lasts far longer on Madeira than in other wine-producing regions of Europe because the fruit ripens at different times, depending upon the altitude. The harvest is a family affair and the pickers set to work from the middle to the end of August. They start with the sweet grape varieties, grown on the lower slopes, and work upwards to the sercial vines, grown for the driest wines, at around 700m (2,300ft).

They then return to sea level to end the harvest in early November, picking the muscatel grapes whose sugars have now been concentrated by the sun. If you are travelling round Madeira in the autumn it is difficult to miss the trucks laden with grapes bound for the factories of Madeira's leading wine producers.

Local people do not wait the 20 years or so that it takes to produce fine Madeira, and thus a certain

Madeira is known for the quality of wine produced

Madeiran grapes represent a major source of income and are picked with care

harvest. Now everyone can relax and enjoy the fruit of their labour. Visitors to Madeira can enjoy the fruits without the hard work – Funchal hosts a month-long wine festival in September, which is good fun, even if it is put on *para o inglês ver* (literally 'for the eyes of the English', that is, for the benefit of tourists). For a taste of the real thing, head for Estreito de Câmara de Lobos, 20km (12¹/₂ miles) west of Funchal, the island's vineyard capital – here you can watch the harvest and take your pick from a number of bars and restaurants serving the local wines.

amount of the harvest goes into the production for purely local consumption of fruity wines such as *canina* (from Estreito de Câmara de Lobos), *jaquet* (from Seixal and Porto Moniz) and *americana* (from Porto da Cruz). A little of this wine is still produced the traditional way, for old times' sake, by treading the grapes in a stone or cement tank called a *lagar*. Most of the grapes, however, are put through a stainless steel, electric-powered press.

The juice is placed in barrels and left to ferment – local wine is drunk very young and the first batch will be ready for tasting in early November, coinciding with the end of the

Old Blandy Wine Lodge has been a winery since 1840

Monte's revered church

Crowned Emperor of Austria and King of Hungary in 1916, he was deposed in 1918 and exiled first to Switzerland and then, at his own request, to Madeira. He did not live long on the island, dying of a sudden attack of pneumonia in 1922, aged 35, leaving a wife and several children.

6km (3³/₄ miles) north of Funchal. Monte Palace Tropical Gardens open: Mon–Fri 9am–6pm, Sat 9am–5pm. Admission charge. Monte church open: daily 9.30am–1pm & 3–6pm.

Terreiro da Luta

On the hillside just above Monte is the spot known as Terreiro da Luta, marked by a statue of the Virgin standing on top of a 5.5m- (18ft-) high column. It was in this spot that the little statue of the Virgin, revered in the church at Monte, appeared miraculously to a shepherd girl in the 15th century. The present statue dates to 1927, when it was erected in fulfilment of a vow made by devout Madeirans during the bombardment

(*Cont. on p74*)

The Monte toboggan

It is de rigueur to make the descent back to Funchal by toboggan, a method of transport that has thrilled and intrigued visitors to Madeira for nearly 150 years.

Ernest Hemingway, not a man given to expressing strong emotions, described the toboggan ride from Monte to Funchal as one of the most exhilarating experiences of his life. Sliding in a wicker basket on wooden runners over the polished cobbles, toboggans can at times reach considerable speeds, though the drivers, with their rubber-soled boots for grip, ensure that corners are negotiated safely. Sadly, the high cost of maintaining cobbled roads is encouraging the increased use of tarmac and the descent of the toboggans over certain sections of the run is becoming perceivably slower as a result.

Madeiran tobogganing as a method of transport was invented around 1850, though horse- and bullock-drawn sleds were in use well before then. Some visitors consider this the essential Madeiran experience. You can go all the way to Funchal on a 4km (2$\frac{1}{2}$-mile) ride, lasting 20 minutes, for around €13.50 per person (two people per sled), or take the shorter run to Livramento (2km/1$\frac{1}{4}$ miles; 10 minutes) for €10 per person.

The Monte toboggan

of Funchal by a German submarine in 1916.

During World War I the Germans sought to end Madeira's use as a supply base for Atlantic shipping by sending in a submarine which first sank a number of ships moored in Funchal's harbour and then shelled the city itself.

Appealing to the Virgin of Monte for protection, pilgrims promised to erect a statue in her honour. The bombardment ceased and Funchal survived the rest of the war unscathed, so grateful Madeirans created the present memorial. Round the foot of the monument is a symbolic rosary, made from the anchor chains salvaged from those Allied ships sunk in the harbour by German torpedoes.

Tropical plants add exotic interest to a garden that is essentially English in style

Quinta do Palheiro
Blandy's Gardens

These gardens were first laid out in the 19th century by the original owner, the wealthy Count of Carvalhal, but his heirs proved profligate with their inheritance and the estate was purchased from them by the Blandy family in 1885. Successive generations of the Blandy family have tended the garden, which is an interesting blend of English-style design and tropical planting.

Of all Madeira's gardens, this one is the most rewarding. If you follow the Gardens and *levadas* walk (*pp76–7*), you can combine a morning spent here with a visit to Hortensia Gardens Tea House and Funchal's Jardim Botânico for a day of horticultural indulgence.

If you arrive by car, you can drive from the ticket office at the entrance to the car park by the house, but walkers will enjoy the stroll down the cobbled drive where trees are interspersed with camellias, and massed agapanthus line the avenue – and the view to the left is one of hay meadows and woodland, a scene that could almost be in England.

Blandy's Gardens are located 550m (1,804ft) above sea level, so it is cool and moist enough for oak, beech and chestnut trees to thrive. These were not planted by the Blandy family but by the count, who adored the English landscape.

At the bottom of the drive, signposts direct you to a sunny terrace below the house, hung with scented jasmine, roses and other climbers. In the beds below, butterflies dart about amid colourful salvias and verbenas.

From the centre of the terrace there is a stone staircase, flanked by flame-shaped Italian cypress trees and terracotta urns, which gives a good view of the house (not open to the public). Below the staircase is a wide path lined with rare and unusual trees, such as the sweet-scented magnolia-like *Michelia doltsopa* and the ancient gnarled *Hagerstromia indica*, a Chinese tree which sheds its bark to reveal fresh colours beneath.

Midway down this central walk, a path to the left leads to a bridge across a frog-filled pond, and to a little chapel built in restrained baroque style by the Count of Carvalhal. Beyond the chapel is a magnificent long border modelled on the typical English herbaceous border – but planted with spectacular abutilons, angel's trumpet (*Datura sanguinea*) and other tender plants among the blue delphiniums and multicoloured sweet peas.

The most beautiful part of the garden comes next: the Ladies' Garden, a serene spot where you can bask in the sunlight while enjoying the birdsong and looking out over hedges clipped to the shape of peahens sitting in their nests. The topiary forms are created out of *Muelenbeckia*, an Australian plant similiar to box, that lends itself well to clipping into intricate designs.

Among the striking plants here is a wonderfully gnarled *Saphora japonica* tree fringed by a cascade of branches

Striking flowers and foliage are guaranteed all year round

sweeping down from the crown to the ground. Another plant is a *Sparmannia africana* whose simple white flowers open to reveal wonderful yellow and scarlet stamens, much visited by bees.

A path to the right of the Ladies' Garden leads out through a low iron gate into a long alley of plane trees and up to the Count of Carvalhal's 18th-century house, which is fronted by giant holm oaks and three deep-water troughs colonised by frogs.

Beyond the house is woodland, and eventually you get back to the formal gardens. A signpost points left towards *Inferno* (Hell), but, far from being hot, the woods are cool, wet, shaded and full of graceful tree ferns and masses of vivid blue trailing morning glory vine.
8km (5 miles) northeast of Funchal, off the ER102 Camacha road.
Open: Mon–Fri 9.30am–4.30pm.
Admission charge.

Walk: Gardens and *levadas*

This walk follows part of the important Levada dos Tornos, one of the most important of Madeira's levadas. Completed in 1966, it is 106km (66 miles) long. This section passes through wooded slopes opening up at times to give some great views across Funchal. Do not be put off by the scruffiness at the start of the walk; it is an urban levada *and does get much better.*

You should allow at least 2 hours for just the walk, and an entire day if you want to spend time in the gardens.

The walk is manageable if you are physically fit, do not suffer from vertigo, and are accustomed to walking and climbing steep inclines. A must is a pair of well-proven walking shoes with a good grip for muddy areas. A walking stick will help. Wear light clothing, a hat and sunblock, and bring water. It is not a good idea to walk the levadas *alone: go with a group or a tour guide recommended by the tourist office.*

Quinta do Palheiro

The walk begins at the Quinta do Palheiro (*see pp74–5*), 8km (5 miles) northeast of Funchal and reached by bus 37 or taxi.

To the Levada dos Tornos

This *levada* will take you to the Jardim Botânico (Botanical Garden). To get to the *levada*, turn right out of the Quinta do Palheiro gates, and follow the straight road running alongside the *quinta* wall. At the top of the hill (after 400m/1,300ft) is a junction with a couple of cafés: turn left and walk up the slope. At the crest, turn left to follow a side wall of a white warehouse, with the sports stadium high up on your right: the *levada* starts behind the warehouse.
Following the levada *footpath you will see a local school.*

To Hortensia Tea House

The *levada* path passes through a mimosa wood and shortly afterwards meets the ER102 road with a sweeping view over Funchal. This is an urban *levada* and some early stretches have rather more litter and noise than you would want to encounter – it does, however, soon get much better. Cross the road and continue on the *levada* path through pine and mimosa woods, with wonderful views to the left of the Quinta do Palheiro and the golf course.
Continue for 1km (²/₃ mile) until you meet the ER201 road.

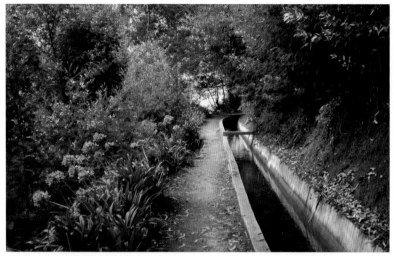
Levada dos Tornos is easy to walk

Crossing the ER201 you will come to the most enchanting part of the walk as the *levada* twists and turns through a eucalyptus wood, heading up a narrow valley and back along the other side.

You will soon come to the Hortensia Gardens Tea House, justly famous for its apple pie, a lush landscaped garden which hides a delightful tea room set on terraces and in a conservatory with views across Funchal. Try some of their renowned apple pie with your tea or coffee – it's delicious.

To the Quinta do Pomar

Enjoy this idyll while it lasts, for you will return to 'civilisation' after 15 minutes. Cross the road and walk past a *levada* station where the flow of the waters is controlled. Shortly after you will reach the Quinta do Pomar; soon after you reach the road and a little neo-Gothic chapel. From here, it is a steep 15-minute walk down to the Botanical Garden. You can, if you prefer, cross the road and continue along the *levada* path for another 15 minutes to Romeiros; here you can catch bus 29 past the Botanical Garden on its way to Funchal.

Jardim Botânico

To get to the Botanical Garden (*see pp61 & 64*), turn left and follow the steep road downhill. Where the main road swings left, carry straight on down the path for a bird's-eye view of Funchal. At the next junction, turn right at the Restaurante Miranda, then take the first left down Caminho dos Voltas. After 10 minutes this leads to the Botanical Garden entrance. From here, take a taxi or buses 29, 30 or 31 down to Funchal, or the cable car to Monte.

Terraces and crops

Madeiran terracing, a monument to human perseverance

The island of Madeira is a human artefact, shaped and sculpted by African slaves until slavery was abolished in 1775, and then by hard-working islanders engaged in backbreaking toil. Tumultuous geological forces formed the island's deep ravines and hidden valleys, but human hands moulded the slopes into stepped terraces, piling up boulders to create retaining walls. Baskets laden with red-brown soil were carried up from the valley bottom – returning the soil that had been eroded by floods and rain after the early settlers had burnt down the tree cover. Little by little the shape of the island was subtly changed, especially on the sunny southern side where the rocks and cliffs absorb sun by day, giving out warmth at night like a radiator. Here, from sea level up to 300m (985ft), every patch of cultivable land is used to grow bananas exported in quantity to mainland Portugal, grapes for wine and for eating, and exotic fruits such as mangoes, avocados, passion fruits and papayas. Higher up, market gardeners produce cabbages, carrots, onions, potatoes and yams in tiny fields interspersed by orchards devoted to citrus fruits, custard apples and figs. Higher still, at 400m to 700m (1,300ft to 2,300ft), it is common to see fruit trees, such as apples, pears, plums and cherries, a delightful sight when in blossom in spring. The fruits are used to make *ginja* (cherry liqueur), *sidra* (cider) and other warming distillations, as well as being sold in Funchal's market. Few edible crops are grown above 700m (2,300ft) in the woodland zone, and this is the point at which the terracing usually stops; even so, good use is made of the fertile volcanic soil for growing eucalyptus, the island's most important timber crop, willows for weaving and bay trees for flavouring beef *espetada*.

The fruits of year-long toil

Eastern Madeira

Wooded slopes of luxuriant vegetation contrast with the arid, windswept and treeless eastern tip, both dramatic in their own way. This is the most developed part of the island. It was once the centre of the whaling industry, but today is the centre of wickerwork crafts. There are several historic towns both on the coast and further inland.

Camacha

Camacha is a village devoted to the production and sale of wickerwork. Almost everyone who lives here is employed in the industry, either as weaver or as vendor. The main building on the village square is the Café Relógio (Clock Café), a multi-storey emporium crammed with wickerwork and often crowded with coach-borne shoppers.

Here you can see a vast range of wickerwork products, from tea trays, plant-pot holders and magazine racks to peacock-backed chairs, bedheads and picture frames – enough, in fact, to furnish every part of the house if you were so minded. Most visitors content themselves with modest purchases – a shopping basket or gardener's trug, for example, which are easier to carry

Madeiran wickerwork on display in Camacha

home by air. The shop will arrange freight forwarding for larger purchases if you wish, but the prices can be steep for bulky items. If you are lucky, you will be able to watch willow weavers at work in the supermarket basement. They work with extraordinary speed, the result of years of practice. Most weavers specialise in one type of wickerwork – be it linen baskets or babies' cradles – and build up a proficiency over time. Just for fun, and to show off their artistic skills, a group

of local weavers created a vast galleon, with billowing sails, and a Noah's Ark, with elephants, lions, monkeys and deer, which is displayed on the middle floor. None of these are for sale, a fact which disappoints some visitors. The **Café Relógio** (*Largo Achada. Tel: (291) 922777*) above the wicker warehouse is the venue for folk nights every Saturday evening when the local dance group, one of the best on the island, gives a spirited performance.

15km (9⅓ miles) northeast of Funchal.

See pp94–5 for route.

Wickerwork

Wickerwork is one of Madeira's most important cottage industries, employing some 2,500 people. The industry dates back to the 19th century when cane furniture was very popular and Madeirans began copying examples imported to the island by British visitors. Today the wicker products sold as souvenirs in Madeira represent only a fraction of the island's total output, most of which is exported to the USA and Europe.

Willows are grown all over the island at heights of 700m to 800m (2,300ft to 2,600ft), where the cloud

Finishing a chair

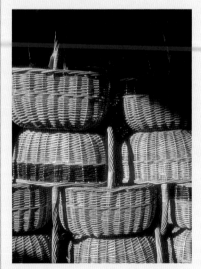

Baskets for sale

tends to hang, providing plenty of moisture. The trees are pollarded by having all their branches cut off at a relatively young age. This encourages the tree to produce lots of new shoots which can grow up to 2m (6¹/₂ft) in length in a single growing season. The shoots are harvested from January to March and left to soak in water before the bark is peeled off. They are then dried, often by being exposed to the sun on the roofs of willow weavers' houses. Before being woven into baskets or furniture, the canes are boiled to make them supple, which turns

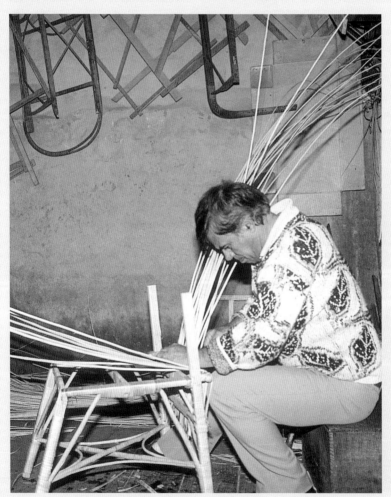

their colour from white to the more familiar brown. Walking around the countryside, you may well see great bundles of willow stacked in the sun, and you may even see weavers at work, seated on low stools outside their houses.

Demonstrations of willow weaving can be seen at Camacha (*pp80–81*), the centre of the industry, where you can also marvel at the bewildering array of different wicker products – from simple place mats to the most ornate birdcages.

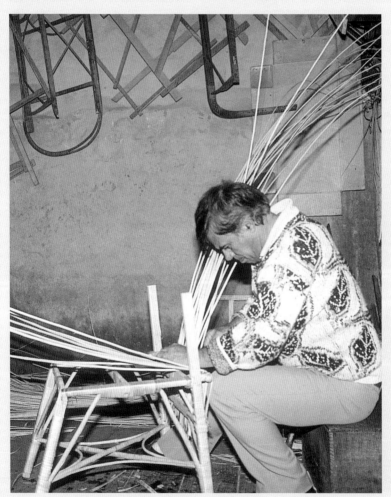

A willow weaver displays his dexterity and skill

Caniçal

Caniçal is a gritty little working port where the fishing community gets on with its business as if the tourists were invisible. Most visitors come here for the Museu da Baleia (Whale Museum) but then find themselves drawn to the nearby beach where it is possible to stand around for an hour or more, watching the boat builders at work or the tuna fishermen bringing in their catch.

The new, rehoused **Whale Museum**, which replaced the older one, features an interesting array of artefacts in an exhibition that chronicles the history of whaling and, in particular, Madeira's involvement in it, up until 1989. At this point Madeira began the transformation from a whaling community to a leader in whale conservation, drawing on the experience and knowledge of the retired Madeiran whalers to understand the movements and habits of the sperm whale in particular. It is hoped that the whales will find sanctuary in the newly established marine reserves off the coast of Madeira. Call ahead to get confirmation of opening hours. *Rua da Pedra d'Eira. Tel: (291) 961859. Admission charge.*

To the east of Caniçal you can see the building that once served as Madeira's

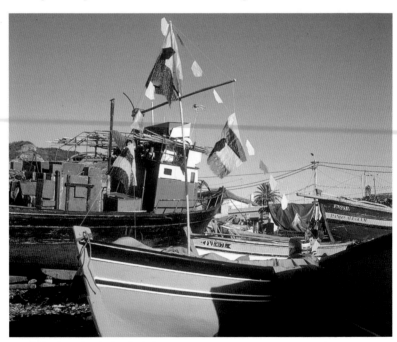

Tuna fishing boats beached at Caniçal

principal whaling station, where whale carcasses were reduced to ivory, oil and ambergris (the waxy lining of the whales' intestines, used in perfume manufacture). Now the building is part of the much bigger free port (Zona Franca) complex, intended to attract overseas investment funds and manufacturing to Madeira.
32km (20 miles) east of Funchal.

Caniço

Caniço is worth a brief visit for its imposing 18th-century baroque church, whose tall bell tower is visible to all motorists as they speed along the road from Funchal to the airport.

Some 2km (1¼ miles) southeast, on the coast at Caniço de Baixo, is the **Roca Mar** resort complex, noted for its diving facilities: there is good diving off the beach here and at the nearby underwater nature park, 4km (2½ miles) west at **Ponta do Garajau**. Literally translated, Ponta do Garajau means 'Tern Point' – so named because early explorers found a large colony of terns nesting on the cliffs below. Today its most prominent feature is a statue of Christ with outstretched arms, smaller than similar statues in Rio de Janeiro and Lisbon, and erected in 1927. The headland commands good views of Funchal, and the sunset can be dazzlingly colourful. If you decide that you want to linger, you can eat back in Caniço, where there is a good choice of several popular restaurants and bars catering to locals and to the

Caniço's church, an architectural masterpiece in grey and white

German visitors who favour the nearby resorts.
9km (5½ miles) east of Funchal.

Machico

After Funchal, Machico is Madeira's second-largest town, with a population of 13,000. The town is divided by the River Machico and sits at the mouth of a fertile green valley backed by mountains. The intensively cultivated terraces clinging to the valley sides show that many local people make their living in agriculture, while there is a small boatyard and fishing harbour on the coast. With the building of several new hotels, Machico is developing as a tourist resort.

Some say that Machico is named after Robert Machin (*see pp16–17*), the English sailor who was shipwrecked on

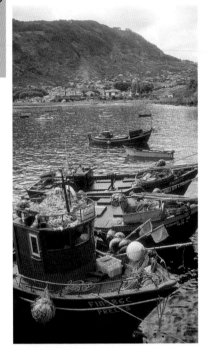

Machico's fishing fleet stands ready for a long night at sea

Igreja Matriz

Teixeira's statue stands in the town's main square, in front of the Igreja Matriz, the parish church of Machico. Though less ornate than Funchal's cathedral, this church is of similar vintage, founded at the end of the 15th century under the patronage of King Manuel I of Portugal and with a handsome Gothic portal.

Cristo Chapel

Older still is the Cristo Chapel, built, according to tradition, on the site of Robert Machin's grave soon after Zarco landed on this spot. Floods have frequently damaged the chapel, which has been rebuilt numerous times, most recently in 1957. Locals call it the Capela dos Milagres (Chapel of Miracles) after the miracle-working crucifix inside – though its miraculous powers are now rarely sought since the chapel is often locked.

Madeira with his companions before the island was officially claimed by Portugal. Zarco is said to have found Machin's grave, marked by a rough cross of cedarwood, when he first landed. Others say that Zarco was moved by homesickness to name the spot after his native town of Monchique on mainland Portugal. Once settlement of the island got under way, Zarco ruled the western part from Funchal, and his fellow navigator, Tristão Vaz Teixeira, as Captain General of the eastern part, ruled from Machico.

Machico is 24km (15 miles) northeast of Funchal.

The crucifix lived up to its reputation in 1803 when floods devastated the chapel. Not long afterwards, an American sailor landed on Madeira bearing the cross – he had spotted it floating on the waves and was eventually able to return it to the rebuilt chapel. The crucifix is carried round the town in a torchlight procession on the nights of 8 and 9 October.

Forte do Amparo and Pico do Facho

Not far from the chapel is the triangular Forte do Amparo, built in

1708 near the seafront to provide Machico with some measure of defence against pirate raids. So devastating were these raids that a constant lookout was kept from the hill to the north of the town, known as the Pico do Facho (Torch Peak). Warning bonfires or beacons were lit if danger threatened, and this practice is remembered every year on the last Sunday in August when a huge bonfire is lit to celebrate the Festa do Santíssimo Sacramento (Feast of the Holy Sacrament). Pico do Facho is easy to reach by road from Machico: take the Caniçal road and turn left just before the entrance to the road tunnel. There are fine views from the summit, with the airport, 4km (2¹/₂ miles) to the southwest, prominent in the foreground and the cliffs of Ponta de São Lourenço in the opposite direction.

Ponta de São Lourenço

The easternmost tip of Madeira does not dip gracefully down to the sea with gentle gradient; true to the tumultuous character of the island's terrain, it stops abruptly at the precipitous edge of several canyon-like cliffs 180m (590ft) or more above sea level. Atlantic waves pound the base of the cliffs, undermining them gradually so that every so often great rocks crash down to join the smashed-up boulders already littered chaotically between the cliffs

(*Cont. on p92*)

Massive cliffs mark the easternmost tip of Madeira at Ponta de São Lourenço

Walk: Ponta de São Lourenço

This 3-hour walk is rigorous but it provides some breathing space on your tour of eastern Madeira. This is a good place to stop off and stretch your legs while exploring the massive cliffs and bays at the tip of the island, enjoying lovely views of the coast.

Developments around Caniçal to create the industrial free port have tamed the landscape as you approach the island's easternmost point, but you will then pass through a lunar landscape of burnt orange and chocolate-brown soils as

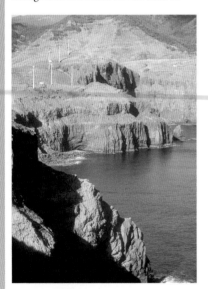

Modern wind turbines contrast with the primeval ruggedness of the volcanic landscape at the island's eastern tip

you approach the end of the tarmac road. Leave the car here and climb the rocks to the right of the car park, to a picnic area with tables and chairs – and a panoramic view of the Baía de Abra, and the Ilhas Desertas (Deserted Isles) in the distance.

The walk

A footpath signposted PR8 by the car park marks the beginning of the walk. Shortly after, the track divides. You should ignore the wide track that leads upwards and straight ahead; instead, bear right and downhill to the bottom of a shallow valley, then up the other side, keeping the wide view of the bay to your right.

As you climb the ridge ahead, the views become more and more dramatic, and the sunshine heightens the vivid colours of the striped cliff-faces on your right, resembling a section through a giant layer cake.

Other rock formations include basaltic extrusions – vertical columns of dark volcanic rock forced up through cracks when molten.

Flora

The dry, thin soil of this headland supports a different mix of plants to other parts of the island, including some noble members of the often-maligned thistle family. You may see *Silybum marianum*, the milk thistle, which has bold white-veined leaves and striking flowers. Another very prickly specimen is the horned, or Mexican, poppy (*Argemone mexicana*), with its big papery yellow flowers and bright orange sap. The most abundant of the thistles here is the prickly cardoon (*Eynara cardunculus*), a relative of the artichoke, with big, sweetly scented flowers, much visited by bees and other insects.

Views

After 20 minutes of strenuous uphill climbing you will reach a drystone wall built of boulders, with a gap for walkers to pass through. Beyond this point bear leftwards, descending gradually across the bare biscuit-coloured bedrock. Before long you will reach a flat area, with views to the left down a rock ravine. Down below, Atlantic waves dash against the raw red cliffs of the island's north face.

If you like, you can take a path to the left that gives access to an even more breathtaking view, but only for those with a head for heights. From here on the path is more easy to follow. It leads eastwards to a ridge on which sits a telegraph pole – you are not aiming for the pole itself, but the rock platform higher up to the left of it.

Here you can sit and admire views that stretch far in every direction. To the east you can see the lighthouse on the tip of **Ilhéu do Farol**, the island at the easternmost tip of Madeira. Further to the right is an eyelet or window in the rocky headland called **Ponta do Furado**, and beyond that the flat-topped Ilhas Desertas are normally visible (if not, local lore says it will soon rain).

This is a very different Madeira from the green, flower-filled interior of the island; bleak and inhospitable but none the less beautiful. Here you can enjoy real solitude, alone with the buzzards, hawks and other birds of prey that you may see wheeling overhead as you return to the car park at the start of the walk.

Marine conservation

Visitors to Ponta de São Lourenço may see old men selling trinkets made of whalebone ivory, the last sad remnants of an industry that is no more, for the hunting and killing of whales finally stopped in Madeiran waters in June 1981. The proposal to turn the waters of the archipelago into a marine reserve for ocean mammals is still to take off for the protection of not just sperm whales, but also dolphins that are still hunted for their meat and the monk seals that are persecuted because they are perceived as competing with Madeira's fishermen for commercial fish stocks.

The monk seal is a rare species on the endangered animals list and can be seen supporting the Madeiran coat of arms. Concern that the local population should not become extinct prompted the Regional Government of Madeira to create a protected area on the Ilhas Desertas, where the last few had retreated to, in 1990. The seals were protected from almost all non-scientific activity and have slowly recovered. In 1998, the colony numbered eight individuals; today there are 35. A monk seal has been spotted sunning itself on the slipway in Funchal harbour and occasionally they can be seen swimming along the south coast.

If the scheme is realised, the sight of sperm whales playing in the waters off Madeira may once again become relatively common. That, at least, is the hope of marine biologists working for the Society for the Protection of Sea Mammals who have been conducting research into whale migration in Madeiran waters since 1985.

As the numbers of whales, dolphins and monk seals increase, many former fishermen and whalers are using their skills to take boatloads of tourists out to see these marine mammals. This generates income for communities that relied on hunting these same animals and as a result contributes further to the conservation of Madeira's marine wildlife. Taking a trip with a knowledgeable guide increases awareness of the plight of the animals and helps create a situation where conservation is placed at the top of the agenda. Furthermore, researchers are being greatly aided by former whaling fishermen, who are now using their knowledge and experience of the sperm whales' habits to help protect the very same creatures that they used to hunt.

With the creation of a marine reserve Madeira has underlined its commitment to conservation.

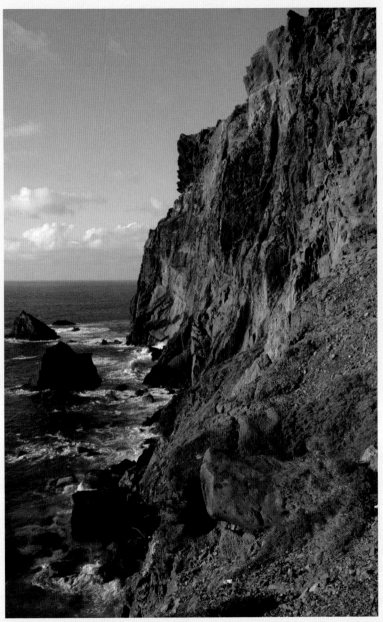

Dramatic cliffs at Ponta de São Lourenço

The tower of São Salvador in Santa Cruz

Senhora de Piedade. Though not large, this is the only beach on Madeira with sand – black sand composed of crushed shells in which you may find tiny fragments of vegetation fossilised by volcanic ash.

32km (20 miles) east of Funchal.

Santa Cruz

It is worth stopping at Santa Cruz even if the former tranquillity of this historic town has been sacrificed to the nearby airport and the busy ER101. The church here, founded in 1533, is one of the least altered on the island, with its bulky bell tower, cross-shaped battlements and Gothic interior. Two other buildings of note nearby are the Town Hall and courthouse, and there is a colourful market on the seafront.

17km (10¹/₂ miles) northeast of Funchal.

Santo da Serra

Santo da Serra occupies a low plateau northeast of Madeira. It has its own microclimate and is often under cloud, rain or mist when nearby Funchal is dry and sunny. Despite this, wealthy city merchants began to build mansions here from the 18th century and the area acquired a reputation as a healthy summer resort.

Today it is best known by sports-loving visitors as the location of a fine golf course (*see p157*) with sea views from the fairways and pine plantations reminiscent of the Scottish Highlands. In the centre of the village is the entrance to an extensive public park

and the sea. If you could see beneath the waves you would discover that the Ilhas Desertas, usually visible offshore to the southeast, are a continuation of the same basic geological formations, though separated by a drowned valley some 100m (330ft) deep. For the romantically inclined this is a spot to savour for its wild and breezy loneliness (*see pp88–9 for a suggested walk*), but when that palls you can take a dip in the more protected **Prainha Bay**, signposted to the south of the 101 road, midway between Caniçal and the end of the road. The beach is reached by means of a steep path near the chapel of Nossa (open daily during daylight hours) which locals know as the camellia garden because of the numerous camellias planted along the main central avenue. The extensive gardens, which once belonged to the Blandy family, also feature tennis courts, a children's playground and some sad-looking deer, ponies, birds of prey and a kangaroo kept within small enclosures. If you follow the main avenue downhill you will come to a viewpoint where you can look out to Ponta de São Lourenço and the easternmost tip of the island.

22km (13²/₃ miles) northeast of Funchal.

The courthouse in Santa Cruz

Drive: Eastern Madeira

The eastern part of Madeira is the most developed, but it also has historic towns and dramatic seascapes. (See p81 for map.)

Although this tour can be done in half a day, take it at a more leisurely pace, perhaps stopping for a picnic or a swim.

1 Quinta do Palheiro

Leave Funchal on the ER101 east; after 3km (1³/₄ miles) turn left on to the ER102, signposted to Camacha. Turn right after 2km (1¹/₄ miles) at the sign for Quinta do Palheiro. Entering, you will feel as if you have been transported to a pristine English garden (*see pp74–5*). The first owner, the wealthy Count of Carvalhal, had a love affair with English landscapes, leading him to include woodland and grassy meadows when the estate was laid out in 1804. In 1885 John Blandy, an English wine merchant, purchased the estate and brought in plants from Japan, China and South Africa. It has been in the same family ever since.

Leaving the *quinta*, turn right, then first left, and then right again to rejoin the ER102. This will take you to Camacha (*see pp80–81*).

2 Santo da Serra

Continue along the ER102 for another 11km (6¾ miles) and you will reach Santo da Serra (*see pp92–3*) with its miniature zoo and extensive park. The road from Santo da Serra is dotted with holiday villas. Turn left after 1.6km (1 mile), then right after 2.2km (1¹/₃ miles), rejoining the ER101 eastwards, signposted to Machico. After 6km (3³/₄ miles), before reaching Machico, turn left on the ER101-3 signposted to Caniçal and the Zona Franca Industrial.

The road passes through a tunnel, then skirts Caniçal, heading for Ponta de São Lourenço: just east of Caniçal is an industrial estate, designed to keep industry out of built-up residential districts. The industrial estate occupies the site of the island's now-redundant whale processing factory (*see p90*).

3 Ponta de São Lourenço

Soon you will pass the industrial zone, and return to volcanic rocks in various shades of orange and brown. A sign to the right, after 1.5km (1 mile), points to Prainha, the location of the island's only naturally sandy beach, a place for swimming in the turquoise-coloured seas.

At the end of the road, you can walk out along the rugged headland of Ponta de São Lourenço (*see pp88–9*) for wonderful views. In the car park, two old men may be selling trinkets made from discarded whalebone. To learn more about this now defunct industry, visit the whaling museum in Caniçal (*see p84*).

4 Machico

A short drive back along the ER101-3 will bring you to Machico (*see pp85–7*), the ancient capital of the eastern part of the island, now a buzzing resort town. Worth visiting is the Manueline-style parish church and the peaceful cemetery just downhill from the Dom Pedro Baía hotel, which has been colonised by some of the island's most spectacular flowers.

5 Santa Cruz

The road from Machico to Santa Cruz passes under the airport runway and if a plane is coming in, it may seem as if it is about to land on your car roof!

In Santa Cruz (*see p92*), the tower of the 16th-century parish church beckons; it is joined on the same square by the equally ancient Câmara Municipal, or Town Hall.

6 Caniço

The last stop before you return to Funchal, Caniço (*see p85*) looks like a developed resort, but you should continue down to the coast at **Ponta do Garajau**, not so much for the outsize statue of Christ as for the beach area with its views, its coloured rocks and the stands of prickly pear cactus. From here, turn left at the first junction to rejoin the ER101 Funchal road at Cancela.

The colouration of the exposed sandstone and volcanic rock in Ponta de São Lourenço makes the area different from the rest of Madeira

Drive: Eastern Madeira

Central Highlands

The deep ravines and bare volcanic rock of the high peaks are Madeira's scenic grandeur at its best. Levada *walks take you deep into the mountains to some of the best views to be had on the island. There is evidence too of the harsh and unforgiving way of life that was, until fairly recently, the lot of many Madeirans.*

Boca da Encumeada

The Encumeada Pass is famous for its views, but it really is pot luck whether the views will be of clouds or of deep green valleys at the time of your visit. The pass is at an altitude of 1,007m (3,304ft), and the clouds tend to hang at the 800m (2,600ft) level, so you may be bathed in sunshine even if the view below is obscured. On a clear day you can see the sparkling blue seas of the south coast, and then turn round 180 degrees to see the wilder grey seas of the north. To the west is the flat top of the Paúl da Serra plateau and to the east are the great peaks and ridges of the central mountain range. The steep-sided valleys that lead up to the pass from the south and the north are lush, green and intensively cultivated. Together they form a deep cleft that seems almost to cut the island in two. If you want to linger for a while, try following one of the *levadas* that radiate out from the pass. The best is the **Levada das Rabaças**, which starts opposite (south

of) the restaurant and bar. Wild flowers abound on the first part of the route and there are splendid views to the south. You can continue for 15 minutes or so, to the point where the *levada* divides (the right-hand branch goes into a tunnel with a door). Beyond this point there is less to see; the hillsides are slowly recovering from the destructive forest fires of the early 1990s.
On the ER104, midway between Ribeira Brava and São Vincente, 43km (26¾ miles) northwest of Funchal.

Pico do Arieiro

At 1,810m (5,938ft), this is Madeira's third-highest mountain peak, and its most accessible (*see pp106–7 for a walk*). You can drive from the centre of Funchal to the top in little under an hour. Just before the peak, you will pass a small round-roofed ice house on the left, built in 1800 to store compressed snow which used to supply Funchal's hotels with ice. Snow is a relatively rare occurrence. Most of the time visitors bask in bright sunshine, high above the rainclouds, enjoying views that stretch across the whole of the island. Connoisseurs of the night sky and the dawn light say that you have not lived until you have spent a night on the mountain to view the Milky Way and the shooting stars that rain down in the early hours of the morning, followed by the most spectacular sunrise. Fortunately you do not have to rough it to spend a night on the mountain. The

government-owned *pousada* (guest house and restaurant), just below the summit, provides every modern luxury. *23km (14¼ miles) north of Funchal.*

Pico Ruivo

Just as spectacular is the sunrise viewed from Madeira's highest peak, the 1,862m (6,109ft) Pico Ruivo. Unfortunately, this mountain summit is much less accessible, but you can walk

See pp100–101 for orange route, pp116–17 for purple route.

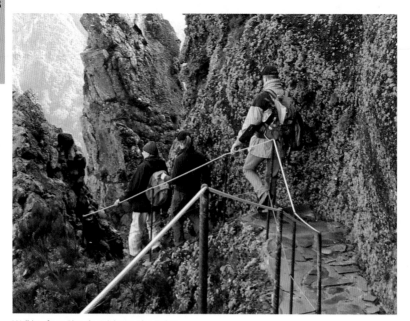

Walking from Pico do Arieiro to Pico Ruivo

to it along the well-marked path from its smaller neighbour, Pico do Arieiro (*see also pp106–7*), provided that you have a head for heights and the time (allow 3 hours each way). Alternatively, you can drive from Santana to Achada do Teixeira, and walk the final stretch up the eastern flank of the mountain (allow 45 minutes each way). There are glorious views over the northeastern coast along the route and from the peak.

45km (28 miles) north of Funchal via Santana.

Poiso

The pass at Poiso is a favourite stopping-off point for walkers and travellers exploring the high peaks of the island's interior because the Abrigo do Poiso restaurant on the crossroads is a welcoming place, with a log fire to comfort chilled or wet bodies. The same fire is used for grilling delicious beef *espetadas*. Poiso sits on the eastern edge of the **Montado do Barreiro National Park**, an area of woodland and open moors, threaded by a tortuously winding narrow road (only open 8am to 7pm). Experiments in reafforestation are being carried out here to give this part of Madeira back its original wooded outline and produce commercially valuable timber. Maritime pine, eucalyptus (Tasmanian blue gum), Douglas fir, Lawson cypress, Japanese red cedar and Indian silver fir are the principal trees being planted.

Wild ponies, wild boar and rabbits are found here – all said to be the descendants of animals imported by early settlers. Rabbits have become such a nuisance that hunting is allowed on Thursdays and Sundays in September, October and November – it is best not to wander off the beaten track on these occasions because of the danger of stray shots. Barbecue pits, spring-water taps and picnic tables are scattered round the park, and on summer weekends Madeirans love to come here to camp.

Small patches of natural Madeiran vegetation can be found within the remoter valleys of the park, a tiny fraction of the dense woodland that covered the island until it was burnt and felled by the early colonisers. Madeirans call these patches of indigenous woodland the *lauri silva*, meaning 'laurel woods'. The laurels concerned are the *Laurus azonica*, which is a type of bay tree, and the Canary laurel (*Apollonius barbajuna*), both tough low-growing evergreens with leathery leaves. These are usually found growing in association with the *til* tree (*Ocotea foetens*), whose flowers have a sharp penetrating scent, and the *vinhático* (*Persea indica*), used by the early settlers for furniture making and known as Madeiran mahogany for its colour and hardness.
10km (6 miles) north of Funchal.

Ribeiro Frio

Most tour buses stop at Ribeiro Frio on the way to Santana, hence the size of the souvenir shop that dominates this little forest resort. The principal attraction is a trout farm, set in a pretty garden, with several concrete tanks fed by the fresh waters of the Ribeiro Frio (literally 'Cold River'), from which the place gets its name.

There is a limit to how long anyone can remain interested in the antics of thrashing rainbow trout, but if you have time to kill you can try exploring one of the nearby *levada* paths. These start just below Ribeiro Frio's bar and restaurant, and are signposted. To the right is the path to Portela: for experienced walkers, this 12km
(*Cont. on p105*)

Fragrant eucalyptus, introduced from Australia as a source of timber

Tour: Curral das Freiras

Curral das Freiras means 'Nuns' Refuge', or 'Valley of the Nuns'. The name derives from the fact that the nuns of Santa Clara convent (see pp38–9) fled here in 1566 to escape from pirates who were attacking the city. The green and unspoilt valley retains a sense of remoteness and other-worldliness even now, despite the number of visitors who come here. (See p97 for map.)

Allow half a day.

The best route out of Funchal is to head north along the Rua Dr Pita from Reid's Hotel then north on the ER107.

1 São Martinho

Stopping off at São Martinho, you can take in the fine views from the terrace in front of the massive modern church (built 1930–52). Inside, in a room to the right of the main altar, is a small museum which doubles as a Sunday school. The exhibits include a silver processional cross and 18th-century garments, embroidered in gold, made for dressing up the religious statues on special feast days.

Take the 107 north, crossing the expressway and follow signs to Pico dos Barcelos.

2 Pico dos Barcelos

From São Martinho northwards the views improve as you climb to this second viewpoint, located at 364m (1,194ft); several restaurants with terraces have been built here to take advantage of the views back to Funchal. Beyond this peak, take the ER107 road, following the narrow winding road to Curral das Freiras as it climbs to the eastern side of the Socorridos Valley, passing through eucalyptus woods.

Ignore the long tunnel that takes you directly to Curral das Freiras. Keep left on the old 107, which continues to climb to Eira do Serrado.

3 Eira do Serrado

Before descending to Curral das Freiras, it is worth diverting to this 'eagle's nest' or eyrie, to look down on the village which forms the end point of the journey. To reach the viewpoint, you first have to walk through a car park where stallholders will try to sell you T-shirts or locally made *ginja* (cherry liqueur). Once through this barrage, you follow a path through sweet chestnut woods which are alive with dancing butterflies when the trees are in flower. The view from the *miradouro* is breathtaking and it reveals why some guides describe the valley as a crater – from this position you get the impression of being on the edge of a great cauldron, completely surrounded by towering cliffs and jagged peaks. This natural amphitheatre magnifies the sounds so well that you can hear every dog bark and cock crow in the tiny village far down below.

4 Curral das Freiras

The final descent to the village follows a road that was not built until 1959 and which passes through several rock-cut tunnels. The old footpath linking the village to the outside world still exists, wide and grassy, zigzagging down the hillside – you can see the start of the path on the left after you emerge from the first tunnel. Once in the village the traditional thing to do, especially if you have walked all the way, is take coffee and eat the local speciality, warm chestnut bread, in one of the bars on the narrow main square. The Nuns' Valley Restaurant is regarded as the best bar – perhaps because the owner makes and sells his own *licor de castanha*, a liqueur that tastes like chestnut-flavoured gin, which he sells by the bottle or glass. If you come here on a Sunday, there will normally be a street market in full swing. If not, you can walk on down the main street to the bottom of the valley and enjoy the peace of this favoured spot, basking in the sunshine and surrounded by dramatic scenery.

20km (12¹/₂ miles) north of Funchal.

Locked away in its own secret valley is the Nuns' Refuge, now a thriving village

Volcanic rocks

Standing on the top of Pico do Arieiro, the view in every direction is of classic volcanic rock formations, enough to send a geologist into paroxysms of excitement. Even to the non-specialist the parched, sponge-like rocks in spectacular colours such as purple, orange, chocolate and red speak of tumultuous volcanic events.

The central mountains of Madeira are made up of solidified lava and ash which began to form beneath the sea in the Miocene Era, 20 million years ago, gradually building up until the lava broke the water's surface, forming a small conical island. Further eruptions then spilled lava down the eastern and western flanks, resulting

Not much can grow near the peaks of Madeira's mountains

The view from Pico do Arieiro

in the present elongated shape. Massive earth movements also played a part, tilting, squeezing and crushing the layers of solid rock, so that you can see cliffs on Pico do Arieiro where different-coloured strata are squashed and folded into bizarre concertina shapes. Hot lava continued to push through joints, gaps and weak points in the rock, so that you will also see great columns and beds of hard basalt interlayered with softer tufas and compressed ash. When all the volcanic activity ceased about 1.7 million years ago, the weathering began – rain and river erosion created the island's spectacular ravines and knife-edge ridges cutting deep into the weakest, softest rocks and leaving the hard rock still standing.

As a result Madeira now consists of a central spine, composed of lofty mountains, the remains of the original volcanic peaks, and numerous deep valleys running off to the north and south, lush with the dense vegetation that Madeira's climate and the fertile soil combine to support.

Turning trout, Ribeiro Frio

($7^1/_2$-mile) walk is well worth doing – it is considered one of the best walks on the island, but it does involve negotiating rock-cut tunnels and steep drops. Just about anybody could manage the first 15 minutes or so of the walk, however, which passes through an area of virgin laurel and heath woodland, typical of the vegetation which covered Madeira until clearance began in the 15th century.

A little further down the road from the bar is another signpost to the left labelled *Balcões* (meaning 'balconies'). After following this *levada* for 20 minutes you will reach the viewpoints to which the name refers, high above the valley of Ribeira da Ametade. The panoramic views take in the high peaks of Madeira's central mountain range to the west, and the lumpy outline of Eagle Rock (Penha de Águia) on the northeast coast.

14km ($8^2/_3$ miles) north of Funchal.

Santana

The lush valleys around Santana, the uncrowned capital of the north, are among the most beautiful and unspoilt on Madeira. In contrast with Funchal and the urbanised south of the island, Santana is undeveloped, a place where traditional Madeiran life continues unaffected by the modern world and where the intensively cultivated and terraced landscape is like a cross between Bali and the Alps.

You will have plenty of opportunity to observe the local agriculture as you journey to Santana, passing fields where cabbages, carrots, potatoes, yams and maize are grown, yielding two or even three crops a year. The roadsides and every patch of uncultivated land are ablaze with the crimson of red hot poker (known as 'fire flowers' in Portuguese), agave, poinsettia, fuchsia, nasturtiums or monbretia, depending on the time of year.

Thatched cowsheds (*see pp114–15*) dot the valley sides, and orchards provide apples, pears, plums, cherries, figs and mulberries. When you add to this the luscious blackberries, loganberries, strawberries and grapes, all grown locally, you will understand why the people of the region are nearly self-sufficient in food.

Santana is famous for its A-framed houses (*see pp114–15*). Right in the centre of the village is a house of this type open to visitors, inevitably part of a souvenir shop and restaurant complex, yet worth a look since it is authentically furnished and will give you an idea of how comfortable these houses can be.

You will see plenty of authentic examples as you wander along the village lanes, genuine lived-in houses set in impeccable gardens. These houses are often interspersed with tiny fields where barley and wheat are grown before being cropped by hand – partly for flour and animal feed, but also for thatching straw to keep the roofs repaired.

Santana is a good place to stop for lunch, since the main restaurant, the

(*Cont. on p108*)

Walk: Mountain peaks

You can drive to the summit of Madeira's third-highest peak, Pico do Arieiro (1,810m/5,938ft), in under an hour from central Funchal. Once there, the magnificent panoramas will tempt all but the most lethargic to take a walk.

The 3-hour walk from here to Madeira's highest peak, Pico Ruivo (1,862m/6,109ft), is rated one of the most spectacular on Madeira. The going is steep, but most relatively fit walkers will manage the route. Those suffering from vertigo should not attempt this walk beyond Viewpoint One. Be sure to check the weather forecast before setting out. Non-slip shoes or trainers are essential and you will also need a sweater and/or a windproof jacket in the winter months. The walk begins to the left of the pousada and is marked by a big yellow sign saying 'Pico Ruivo 10km' (6 miles).

1 Pico do Arieiro

You can spend the night on the summit of this mountain if you book in advance at the **Pousada do Pico do Arieiro** (*tel: (291) 230110*), the government-owned inn; the advantage is the opportunity to watch the sunset, gaze at the night sky away from the glare of city lights, and then observe the most spectacular dawn. Even if you do not make it here early enough for sunrise, you can get a taste of its colours at most times of the day because the sunlight, playing on the orange, purple, pink and brown volcanic rocks, makes their colours all the more intense.

2 To Viewpoint One

The first part of the walk follows a paved path, and the principal ingredients are silence (except for the wind) and spectacular views of deep cliffs and ravines on every side. The eerie silence continues as you approach the first *miradouro*, or viewpoint, and the sense of isolation is increased by the clouds that often cling to the valleys way beneath your feet, cutting you off from the sights and sounds of the noisy, busy world below. The view from the first *miradouro* is dominated by the long ridge of **Pico das Torres** (Peak of the Towers) to the north – so called because of the tower-like lumps and columns running up the jagged ridge to Madeira's second-highest peak (1,851m/6,073ft).

3 To Viewpoint Two

The path now curls round, taking you to the western, and more sheltered, side of a cliff. A few disc-shaped house leeks growing out of the cinder-like rock cling to the cliff. Here you overlook the great gorge of **Ribeira do Cidrão**. In the distance, ahead and to the left, is the great plateau of the **Paúl da Serra** rising above the clouds, marked by giant electricity-generating windmills with their huge propeller blades.

If you suffer from vertigo, this is probably as far as you should go. The 10-minute walk to the next viewpoint is very steep and at times the path is no more than a 2m- (6^{1}/$_{2}$ft-) wide spine of rock, with sheer drops on either side – though there are iron railings and wire ropes to hold on to.

From the second *miradouro* you can see Pico Ruivo to the left, while Funchal, 22km (13^{2}/$_{3}$ miles) away, may just be visible on a clear day. Turning round, far above you can see Pico do Arieiro, where you will now return. Alternatively, you can continue on to the top of Pico Ruivo, though it is best to have a guide for the rest of the route.

A narrow section of the path

São Vicente's Old Town district tempts travellers to stop

O Colmo, and many others serve fine locally produced food, including fresh trout from the farm at Ribeiro Frio (*see pp99 & 105*) and delicious goat's cheese with honey.

The **Madeira Theme Park** is a new attraction in Santana that defies categorisation. It is part open-air museum, part playground, part garden and part exhibition centre. Despite this, it works well, appealing to all the family. All the attractions are devoted to Madeira's history and culture in some way. There are rides, a maze and play areas for children scattered among the typical Madeiran buildings that include the traditional *palheiros*, workshops showing the traditional crafts like embroidery and wickerwork, a Porto Santo windmill and a *levada* with a watermill.

The main attractions are the exhibitions which cover the formation of the island, its geology and discovery. Far from being dry and academic, these are fun and interactive. Some are more akin to fairground rides, including a boat trip through a sound and light show on the discovery of the islands or a simulator to give you full-on experiences of Madeira (including the famous Monte toboggan run) that are very realistic.

The gardens throughout the park showcase Madeira's flora.
Estrada Regional 101, Fonte da Pedra. Tel: (291) 570410. Open: Jun–Sept & 14 Dec–11 Jan daily 10am–7pm; 12 Jan–May & Oct–13 Dec Tue–Sun 10am–7pm. Admission charge.

Santana environs

From Santana you can take the inland road northwards to **Queimadas**, the starting point for several spectacular *levada* walks, including the one that goes to the well-named **Caldeirão do Inferno** (Hell's Cauldron). You can also continue to the end of the same road and walk up to the top of Madeira's highest peak, **Pico Ruivo** (*see pp97–8*).

On the journey back to Santana, the view is dominated by the flat-topped **Penha de Águia** (Eagle Rock), a mountain-sized rocky outcrop which separates **Faial** and **Porto da Cruz**. These two villages are typical of the little port towns that thrived in the era before motorised transport, when boats were used to carry goods around.

Porto da Cruz is a well-preserved example of a port town, with its ancient Roman-tiled houses and stone-built harbour. Few boats use it now, but the local children come here to dive and swim in the deep clean water, well sheltered from the powerful force of the Atlantic waves.

São Vicente

Most visitors to Madeira have to pass through São Vicente at some time because it is located at the junction of the island's spectacular north coast road and the main road to Ribeira Brava in the south. In an attempt to persuade travellers to stop and even stay a night or two, considerable sums have been spent on building new hotels and restaurants, and smartening the town up, so that it sparkles with an almost-too-pristine cleanliness, its buildings whitewashed to dazzling brightness.

(*Cont. on p112*)

The little chapel in São Vicente

Walk: Levada do Furado (Ribeiro Frio to Balcões)

This 1.5km (1-mile) walk is intended as an introduction to levada *walks and is suitable for most people, with the only vertigo-inducing part being the viewpoint at the end. The route is wet underfoot in parts so a good pair of non-slip walking shoes is essential. Remember to take water with you.*

Allow 1½ hours in addition to any time spent at the viewpoint.

Start below the souvenir shop in Ribeiro Frio.

Woodland

Almost opposite the start of the PR10 walk, Levada do Furado to Portela, look for the sign PR11 Balcões. The path is actually a continuation of Levada do Furado. This *levada* was one of the first acquired by the government in its attempt to regulate and distribute the water of the island more fairly. It is a dry *levada* with a wide path beside it passing through mixed woodland of laurel trees, Madeira mahogany and blueberry along with non-native trees such as the oak and the plane tree. At the begining the *levada* runs parallel to the ER103, which rapidly drops away to the right. *Soon the* levada *swings away from the road winding round the mountainside and across a stream.*

Shortly the levada and path pass through a narrow cutting in the rock where the ground can be slippery and wet. Ferns and mosses cling to the dripping rock face above the path. Soon after is a small souvenir shop selling, among other things, the woollen hats with earflaps common in Madeira and ideal for walkers who are surprised by the rapid changes in the weather that Madeira's mountains can throw at you. There is also a tiny bar here where you can buy all the usual drinks and snacks. The *bolo de mel* served here is excellent and a good source of energy.

To Balcões

The path continues along the side of the Ribeiro Frio Valley before turning abruptly left through another cutting in the towering basalt into the parallel valley of the Ribeira da Metade. Soon after is a fork where the *levada* goes to the left. This way is prohibited to walkers, who should take the path to the right. This leads you to the Balcões (literally 'balconies'), a rocky tor and ledge with some spectacular views. Look out across the valley of the Ribeira da Metade, taking in the peaks of the central massif including Pico do Arieiro and Pico Ruivo to the west and the outline of Penha de Águia (Eagle Rock) on the north coast near Faial and Porto da Cruz. The ancient laurisilva forest is important as a water producer. In the manner of a 'cloud forest' the abundant mist of the Metade Valley condenses on the leaves of the trees and falls to the ground to feed the many streams, rivulets and eventually the Ribeira da Metade. From the *miradouro* the reservoir and hydroelectric plant of Fajã da Nogueira, which supplies electricity to the island and water to the municipality of Santana, is clearly visible.

Return the way you came to Ribeiro Frio.

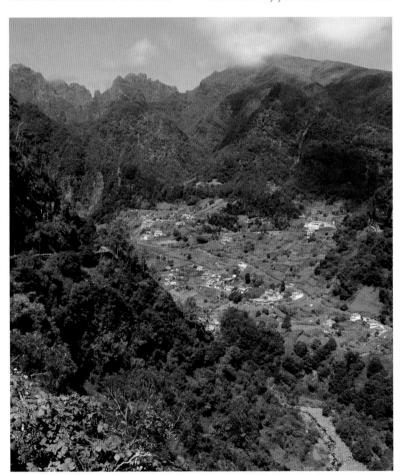

The valley of the Ribeira da Metade with the mountains of the central massif

The Old Town still has considerable charm, with its small, typically Madeiran general stores selling everything from pungent salt cod to religious statues. The simple parish church has colourful tiles and a painted ceiling. The modern church of **Nossa Senhora de Fátima**, with an eye-catching bell tower, and built between 1942 and 1953, stands high on a hill above the town. There is also a tiny chapel built in 1692 by the bridge at the mouth of the São Vicente River, which you will see if you head west towards Porto Moniz on the north coast road.

Not to be missed are the **Grutas de São Vicente** (Caves of Saint Vincent) at the Volcanism Centre, which lies 1km (^{2}/$_3$ mile) up the valley from the Ribeira Brava–São Vicente road. The centre, surrounded by a lovely garden, provides visitors with audiovisual demonstrations of volcanic eruptions and explanations of how islands are formed. The underground caves are the result of an eruption over 400,000 years ago. They are a series of lava tubes measuring over 1,000m (^{2}/$_3$ mile), of which 700m (770yds) can be walked in about 30 minutes.

Multilingual tours are available hourly. The caves, at 40m (131ft) underground, are an easy walk. They were discovered in 1855 by an Englishman, James Johnson. It's doubtful that Johnson would recognise them now as the caves have been brought into the 21st century; for safety reasons they now have electricity, and you can now stand up in them and listen to piped-in music while you explore.

Still, with their dramatic rock pools and streams, and their café-au-lait-coloured walls, the caves are one of Madeira's most popular and beautiful natural wonders.

North coast road

The exhilarating north coast road from São Vicente to Porto Moniz is one of those spectacular pieces of construction at which the Madeirans seem to excel – like the island's *levadas*, construction of the road was a slow manual process of hacking away at the stone to create a narrow ledge in the cliff side, sometimes passing through tunnels.

No machinery or modern technology made the task easier, and that is why the road took 16 years to complete, almost one year for each kilometre of its 19km (11¾-mile) length.

Drive slowly, because the road is only wide enough for one vehicle in places; watch out for oncoming vehicles and be prepared to pull over into a passing place if necessary. While waiting, you can admire the wild seas, the sheer cliffs and the numerous waterfalls which cascade over them, often soaking your car or – as the Madeirans say – giving you a free car wash.

The old road can only be driven in an east–west direction. Take a right turn marked 101 Antiga at the entrance to each tunnel on the expressway.

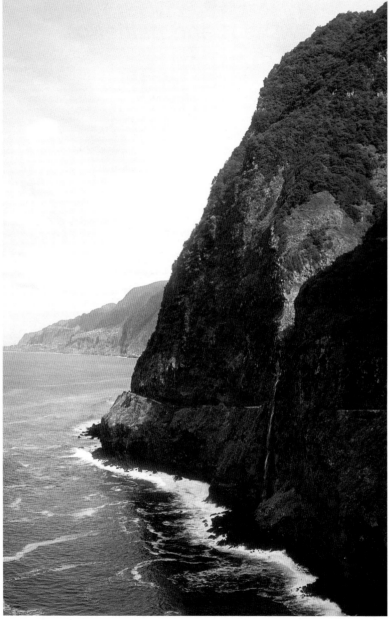

Wild seas, sheer cliffs and cascading waterfalls mark the north coast road

Cowsheds and *palheiros*

What is the difference between a cowshed and a traditional Madeiran *palheiro*, or A-framed house? You may ponder this question as you wander round Santana because in these cases the construction is identical: both have a triangular façade with a thatched roof sweeping from the gable ridge right down to the ground. One answer is that houses usually have pots of trailing geraniums by the door, and the façades are often boldly painted in crimson, white, yellow and blue. The other answer is, of course, that one has human occupants while the other is inhabited by a cow.

Cows in this part of Madeira cannot be left to roam – they would break their legs on the steep slopes, damage the terraces and destroy crops. For their own safety they are kept in a triangular byre: thatched roofs keep them warm in winter and cool in summer. They are milked daily and well looked after; you may see

Palheiros are surprisingly spacious

A *palheiro* looks very similar to a Madeiran cowshed

their owners climbing the hillside beneath a vast pile of grasses and hay with which they are fed. A cowshed is surprisingly roomy inside, like the human version of the *palheiro*.

The *palheiro* house usually has an upper storey, reached by a ladder, for sleeping and storage. Separate toilets are placed away from the house. Meals are prepared out of doors to avoid risk of fire, and prevent the cottage being filled with smoke and cooking smells.

Sometimes you will see sad examples of neglected cottages where the owner has died or moved away. Without constant loving attention the houses soon deteriorate, and the thatch is then replaced by ugly corrugated iron. So far, at least, this has not happened on a wide scale in Santana, and there are government incentive schemes which encourage the older people of the village to maintain their traditional houses and lifestyle.

Drive: Central Madeira

If you have time for only one drive on Madeira, this is the one, taking in burnt volcanic wastes, lush green valleys, wave-battered coasts and traditional island architecture and crafts. (See p97 for map.)

Allow a full day.

Start at Funchal.

1 To Terreiro da Luta

From Funchal, head north out of the city, following Rua 31 de Janeiro (that is, the right bank of the Ribeira de Santa Luzia). Follow the signs to Monte about 5km (3 miles) away (*see pp67–9 & 72*). Continue north on the ER103 for 3km (1³/₄ miles) to Terreiro da Luta, where you can see the statue of the Virgin Mary on a 5.5m (18ft) column, built as a World War I memorial.

2 Pico do Arieiro

After 3km (1³/₄ miles), look for a byroad to the left which takes you through one of the island's national parks – if you miss the turning just go on to Poiso and turn left. Emerging from the park, turn left for 4km (2¹/₂ miles) to reach Pico do Arieiro (*see pp96–7*).

The landscape in the nature park and on the peak is volcanic. Little grows on the rusty red laterite soil, and a major reafforestation programme is underway.

The forestry department faces an additional problem – the number of rabbits which nibble away at the vegetation, including recently planted tree seedlings. At the peak you can take a walk among the magnificent volcanic formations (*see pp102–3*).

3 Ribeiro Frio

Backtrack to Poiso (the Abrigo do Poiso restaurant here is excellent, if you fancy lunch), then take the ER103 left to Ribeiro Frio (*see pp99 & 105*), where you can watch the trout playing in the crystal-clear waters of the local fish farm.

Heading on along the ER103, you will pass through **Achada do Cedro Gordo** – the name referring to the abundant crab apple trees grown for cider production – then through **Cruzinhas**, **Lombo de Cima**, **Degolada** and **Faial**.

This route takes you through gentle agricultural scenery, where the land is highly fertile and local farmers grow produce all year round, harvesting three, or even four, crops of beans, potatoes, carrots, cabbages or maize per year.

4 Santana

The landscape from Faial to Santana is dotted with colourful thatched traditional A-framed houses known as *palheiros* (*see pp114–15*). Many of these are private homes, some are cowsheds; unless you step inside, it is hard to tell the difference between the two as generally they are well kept and beautiful. On an island such as Madeira, with high rocky slopes, cattle can easily fall off if they are left to graze freely, so they are kept in the cool shade of the *palheiros* and their owners bring them bales of fresh grass and hay several times a day.

Santana is fairly ordinary; there's a Town Hall and small church and down on the hillside road there are several pretty squares. What makes it worth a night or two's stop is its location: just above a stunning cable car set along spectacular cliffs within view of glorious mountain scenery.

Surrounding this is some of the most fertile farmland in Madeira, and grape vines, figs, kiwi, mulberries and plums grow in abundance here.

Drive back along the ER101 to Faial; the view is dominated by **Penha de Águia** (Eagle Rock) rising to 590m (1,936ft). The lower portion of the rock is terraced fields; the upper half has been left forested, a perfect home for the ospreys that nest here seasonally. If you are inclined to climb Eagle Rock, the footpaths to the summit are extremely rough; the climb takes about an hour and a half and is not recommended unless you are extremely fit.
Continue on the ER101 to Degolada then take the ER102.

5 Camacha

Following the ER102 for 16km (10 miles) will bring you to Camacha, the centre of the island's wickerwork industry (*see pp82–3 & 147*). This is the best place to purchase souvenirs, and you can watch the weavers.

To return to Funchal from Camacha, take the well-travelled and signposted ER102.

Atmospheric view from Pico do Arieiro

Western Madeira

Everything about the west is dramatic. The high plateau feeds the many rivers that carve out the deep valleys and ravines to the south. To the north the plateau seems to drop straight down into the sea, spilling its water in numerous waterfalls into the Atlantic that pounds those towering cliffs. Amazingly, villages cling to the cliffs and the ever resourceful Madeirans once carved out a road, quite literally, along the north coast.

Calheta

Bathed in sunshine, Calheta is the main village of a sprawling district that thrives on horticulture; its houses with their pretty gardens seem lost in a sea of bananas and vines. Steep cobbled streets lead down to the coast and several of the region's churches have 16th-century features; they include the Chapel of Our Lady of Loreto on the western outskirts of Arco da Calheta, Calheta's own church, with its fine wooden ceiling, and the Reis Magos Chapel at Estreito da Calheta.

One of the most colourful festivals on the island takes place here on 7 and 8 September, when celebrations for the grape harvest and for Our Lady of Loreto become the excuse for decorating the streets with flowers, setting off noisy fireworks and enjoying beef *espetadas*. *On the south coast, 62km (38½ miles) west of Funchal.*

Paúl da Serra

As if to prove that Madeira is not one vast floating flower garden, the Paúl da Serra looms bleakly towards the western end of the island. The name Paúl da Serra means 'Desert Plain', a very apt description for the high plateau where the soil is so thin that only the toughest of grasses will grow.

Even this is cropped tight by goats, sheep and sturdy little cows, and their numbers are strictly limited to prevent all the vegetation from being consumed. Travelling across the plain to Rabaçal or Porto Moniz, you will see caves dug into the sides of embankments to provide shelter for the farmers and for their beasts. You will also see their more modern, but substantially less aesthetic, equivalent, large concrete sheds. Shelter is necessary because it is often very windy up on top of the plateau and this is where the snow will fall, if at all, during the winter months.

A forest of wind turbines has recently been built on the plateau to provide electricity to settlements along the island's north coast, the gleaming white

See pp128–9 for route.

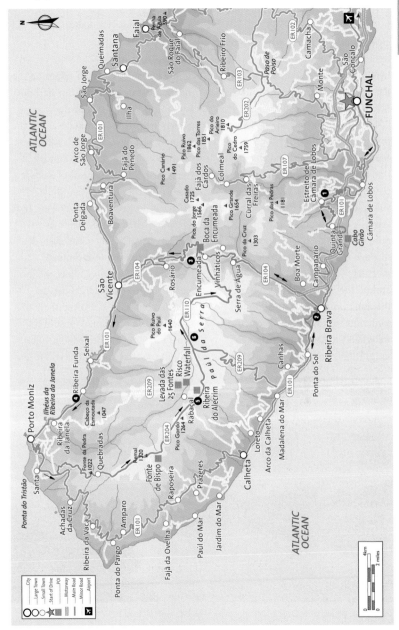

towers and propeller blades looking very high-tech and modern in contrast to the elemental moorland. It is not always wet, windy or misty up here, however, and in summer people come here to camp, play football in the big flat open spaces, and look for the delicious fruits of the bilberry.

The Paúl da Serra also plays a vital role in the island's irrigation system. Rainwater is captured and channelled into reservoirs from which it is fed into power stations and *levadas*. The volcanic rock of the Paúl da Serra also acts as a huge sponge, absorbing rainfall which then filters down through the porous substrata until it meets layers of impermeable clay at around the 1,000m (3,300ft) level. Here the water pours out of the ground, sometimes to cascade as spectacular waterfalls (at Rabaçal, for example, *see p130*) but more often to feed the

island's extensive *levada* network (*see pp142–3*).

60km (37¼ miles) northwest of Funchal.

Ponta Delgada

Ponta Delgada is a small village on the north coast noted for its tiny harbour and for its willow-tree plantations, which provide the raw material for the island's wickerwork industry. The best time to visit is on the first Sunday in September when the Feast of Senhor Jesus is celebrated and the whole village is decked in festive flowers and greenery. The festival celebrates an ancient crucifix which was washed ashore here in the 16th century. Believing it to be miraculous, the local people built a chapel to house the crucifix, but a fire destroyed the building and consumed most of the cross in 1908. Undeterred, the villagers rebuilt the church and they still revere

The unexpectedly flat expanse of moorland on Madeira's high plateau

The red roofs of Ponta Delgada, sheltered by tree-clad hills

the charred cross fragments, which are displayed in a glass case for most of the year.

27km (16¾ miles) west of Santana on the north coast, 60km (37¼ miles) from Funchal.

Ponta do Pargo

Ponta do Pargo is the westernmost headland on Madeira: you can walk out to the lighthouse at the tip for views of the coast, knowing that nothing lies beyond this point except Atlantic waves until America is reached.

If you are interested in wild flowers, you should walk the **Levada Nova**, which runs from Ponta do Pargo to Calheta (a distance of 20km/12¹/₂ miles, but the 101 road with frequent bus services to Funchal is never very far away if you get tired). The combination of moisture and sunshine ensures that the margins of this *levada* have some of the most varied and colourful flowers to be found on the island.

78km (48½ miles) west of Funchal.

Ponta do Sol

Ponta do Sol basks in the sunshine after which it is named: Sun Point is the last village travelling westwards along Madeira's southern coast to receive day-long sunshine – beyond here, cliffs and hills cast shadows in the early part of the day, especially when the sun is low in winter. Exploiting the sunshine to full effect, Ponta do Sol is a major centre of banana cultivation, and there is very little space around the town not covered by plantations: even the cliff faces have tiny terraces which have been hacked out of them and support a few banana plants, as you will see if you follow the coast road – look out for steps cut in the rock face and precipitous paths leading to terraces as you approach the tunnel that leads to Madalena do Mar. The effort of creating and tending such terraces is justified by the extra warmth given out by the rock face at night, storing sunlight by day and acting as a radiator. This helps to ripen the crop earlier in

Even the cinema in Ponta do Sol alludes to the sunshine after which the village is named

His travels eventually brought him to Madeira, where Zarco, the island's discoverer, persuaded him to settle, granting him the land around Madalena do Mar. He founded Madalena do Mar's little church of Santa Catarina in 1457. Knowing nothing of his history, the locals called him Henrique Alemão, or Henry the German.
42km (26 miles) west of Funchal.

Porto Moniz

Porto Moniz is located at the remote northwestern tip of Madeira, about as far as you can get from Funchal, so it is not surprising that until not so long ago there were people in the village who had never seen the island's capital. Even today it feels different from other villages on Madeira, although it has rapidly caught up with the modern world and now boasts several hotels, cafés and restaurants, and the island's only official campsite.

the year, and can mean a premium price if the bananas are ready for sale well before the main crop. Some 600,000kg (590 tons) of bananas are exported from Madeira every year, much of it to Lisbon for sale in mainland Portugal. Ponta do Sol has one of the island's principal packing stations, unmissable because of the stalks piled outside the warehouse beside the main road, waiting to be pulped and processed into animal fodder or glues.

The next-door village of **Madalena do Mar** has an interesting history, for tradition attributes the founding of the village to King Ladislav of Poland. Having been defeated at the Battle of Varna in 1414, Ladislav set off on a pilgrimage round the world, visiting holy sites and doing good wherever he could.

The fresh arrival of roads and electricity has given a boost to the village and opened it up to tourism, but for many villagers the old, slow pace of life continues and few of them own vehicles; walking, often with heavy burdens, is still the norm. Road embankments, built or patched up with concrete elsewhere, are masterpieces of drystone walling around here, and they support a rich flora, covered in succulent house leeks and other wall plants.

The tiny fields are meticulously cultivated, as you will see if you look down on the village from above: there is a fine viewpoint to the north of the village on the ER101. The terraces that tumble down the hillside, and the flat fields around the village itself, are all fenced with dried heather and bracken, creating a low 0.5m (1¹/₂ft) boundary wall which is sufficient to protect the crops from the strong Atlantic winds, driving rain and salt-laden sea spray.

Descending into the village, you will find all the paraphernalia of a seaside resort, including a go-kart track and shops selling buckets and spades, despite the absence of sand. This is all part of a general diversification scheme to help the villagers reduce their dependence on agriculture.

For many visitors, Porto Moniz is the end point of a drive along the spectacular north coast road. It has several excellent seafood restaurants which attract coach parties at lunchtime. For those on a longer stay, there is an unusual swimming pool next to the Residencial Calhau hotel on the edge of the ocean. Natural rock pools in the volcanic rocks have been deepened and linked by concrete pathways: you cannot swim far in the pools, but you can bask in the sun-warmed water while watching the Atlantic waves rolling in and beating against the shore.

75km (46²/₃ miles) northwest of Funchal.

Ribeira da Janela

Just before Porto Moniz, you will catch sight of the *janela* (window) in the offshore rocks, a feature which gives its name to this lush and scenic ravine, which cuts up to Rabaçal and Paúl da Serra.

If you have four hours to spare, a walk up this valley will prove rewarding. Follow the Levada da Central da Ribeira da Janela up from the car park and reservoir just above the village of Lamaceiros.

55km (34¼ miles) north of Funchal.

The unspoilt virgin vegetation of Rabaçal's hidden valley

Rabaçal

Rabaçal itself consists of no more than a government rest house, but the woods around it are among the most scenic on Madeira, supporting an ecological community of ancient laurel and tree heath, and rich in ferns, mosses and lichens, as well as thistles, geraniums and foxgloves in season.

The area is well watered by *levadas*. You can follow paths to the Risco Waterfall, or to the beauty spot known as the **Vinte e Cinco Fontes** (25 Springs), a pool into which scores of little water courses either drip or pour, the volume depending on the time of year and the amount of rainfall. (*See the* Risco Waterfall *walk, pp130–31.*)
65km (40 1/3 miles) northwest of Funchal, on the Paúl da Serra road to Porto Moniz.

Ribeira Brava

Ribeira Brava is a point along the island's southern coast where several roads and paths meet, so it started out as a watering hole where weary travellers would rest before continuing on their journey.

Old habits die hard: even in these times of swift motorised transport, few Madeirans pass through the town without stopping for rest and a cup of coffee. This explains the unusually large seafront parking area, and the large number of nearby bars.

There is a small covered market, a miniature version of Funchal's Mercado dos Lavradores, where fish, flowers, fruit and vegetables are sold.

The name of the village, Ribeira Brava, means 'Wild River'. Most of the year you will search in vain for evidence that the river running to the west of the town deserves such a dramatic name, but heavy rains in autumn can see the water level rise 3–4m (10–13ft), and the bed is strewn with boulders and debris brought down from the mountains by flash floods.

The sea can be equally wild, hence the massive concrete breakwaters piled upon the pebble beach to absorb the force of the waves. You are unlikely to be tempted to swim here, but you may want to explore the little fishing harbour, to the east of the town, through an archway cut in the cliffs.

In the grid of streets stretching north from the waterfront, you will find several characterful shops and typical examples of Madeiran town architecture – houses with ornate balconies and green window shutters.

Ribeira Brava is the starting point for some attractive *levada* walks leading up the valley to the Boca da Encumeada pass. The town has two modern hotels popular with walkers.
32km (20 miles) west of Funchal.

São Bento (St Benedict)

On the main square, São Bento church is one of the most interesting on Madeira, with several features surviving from the original 16th-century building. One of these is the unusual painted stone font, carved with interlaced grapes, pomegranates, cable motifs and

São Jorge

Fruit orchards and willow plantations dominate the scenic valleys between São Jorge and its neighbours, Arco de São Jorge and Boaventura. Tourist buses stop at the big As Cabanas shopping and restaurant complex just outside São Jorge. However, if you are not interested in embroidery and passion-fruit liqueurs you can visit the pretty baroque church in the village, or take a refreshing stroll along the headland to the **Ponta de São Jorge** lighthouse, from where there are extensive views of the wild northern coastline.

Equally good are the views along the coast road to **Boaventura**. Here the main attraction is the peaceful cemetery set high up above the village church; romantic souls come here to visit the grave of Miss Turner, an American lady who died around 1925. Miss Turner was the owner of a thriving tea room catering to English visitors in Santo da Serra, noted for its splendid garden. Her gardener would often talk about his home village of Boaventura, describing it as a paradise by the sea, beyond the Madeiran peaks. His descriptions fed her dreams and, though she never visited the village, she requested that her mortal remains be buried in the Boaventura cemetery, a wish that was respected, even though it meant carrying her coffin over steep mountain tracks, since roads only came to the area in recent years.

50km (31 miles) north of Funchal.

Characterful Ribeira Brava

wild beasts, including wolves. Similar beasts are carved on the base of the wall pulpit and on the capitals of the arches nearest to the high altar. The original altar surround was moved to the left-hand aisle during modernisation work in 1948. It consists of a carved and gilded tabernacle and reredos with a Flemish painting of the Nativity above.

Much of the chancel, painted to resemble marble, is modern, but there is a 16th-century wooden sculpture of the Virgin above the high altar.

Exploring churches

Madeira is still a very religious island, and large sums of money are spent on maintaining and restoring parish churches. Sadly, for the architectural historian, this means that most have been rebuilt several times since their original foundation and the present structures, with their bland neo-baroque façades and interiors, seem to be of no great age. If you dig around, however, you may find features that are older and more interesting. Here are some clues on where to look.

First seek out the font at the back of the church – usually housed in a small room, or baptistery, to the north (left as you enter the church). The font is likely to be the oldest-surviving feature because, although churches have often been rebuilt, the parish will have retained the original 15th-century font as a link with the original community. Some are plain hollowed-

São Bento church in Ribeira Brava dates from the 16th century

Ribeira Brava's Manueline pulpit

showing scenes from the life of Christ are likely to be more modern and mass produced.

Ceilings do not get repainted very often because of the difficulty of access; many were last painted in the early part of the last century, if not earlier, and floral patterns are common, usually incorporating examples of Madeira's abundant wild flora. Every church on Madeira has something of interest if you look hard enough, even if it is not of great age.

A favourite with many visitors is the fishermen's chapel in Câmara de Lobos (*see p67*), whose walls are painted with charmingly naïve pictures of the miracles of St Nicholas, patron saint of seafarers.

out boulders, while others (such as the one in Ribeira Brava: *see pp124–5*) are more ornately carved.

The main altar is likely to be the next oldest feature, and, although the statuary may be modern, the ornate baroque altar surround, often of carved and gilded wood, usually dates to the 17th or 18th century and is full of fascinating little details, such as cherubs and butterflies hidden amid a mass of vine leaves and foliage.

The walls of the church may be covered in *azulejos* (tiles) of similar date – usually hand-painted in soft blues and yellows in complex geometric patterns. Pictorial tiles

The gilded woodwork in Câmara de Lobos's chapel

Drive: Western Madeira

This tour of western Madeira will take you along the sunny southern coast, over the stunning Encumeada Pass, along what remains of the spectacular old north coast road to Porto Moniz before returning over the contrasting moorlands of Paúl da Serra. (See p119 for map.)

Allow two days. It can be made into a one-day tour by missing out the south coast road section and taking the expressway to Ribeira Brava in about 20 minutes.

1 The south coast road

Leave Funchal along the Estrada Monumental (ER229 until you reach the picturesque fishing village of **Câmara de Lobos** (*see pp66–7*) made popular by Winston Churchill. Another 7km (4⅓ miles) and you reach **Cabo Girão** (*see p66*) where you can look down 551m (1,808ft) from one of the world's highest cliffs onto a tiny patch of farmland reached only by boat or the cable car at Fajã das Bebras.

2 Drive to the sun

After 11km (6¾ miles) you arrive in **Ribeira Brava** (*see pp124–5*) where you can stop for a coffee, wander through the market and visit São Bento Church. Take the coast road out of town (ER101) to **Ponta do Sol** (*see pp121–2*), so called because it gets the sun all day; hence bananas growing in every conceivable space. If doing the drive over two days this is the best place to break the tour. *Return to Ribeira Brava to continue the tour.*

3 Over the pass

Take the ER104 out of town heading north for 7km (4⅓ miles) then turn left on the ER228 signposted Serra de Água. This will take you to **Boca da Encumeada** (*see p96*), passing on the way one of the two government-owned *pousadas* on Madeira, a pass and the viewpoint where two deep valleys are separated. It is the starting point for several *levada* walks.

Take the road down into the northern valley and to **São Vicente** (*see pp109 & 112*) and the eastern end of the north coast road to **Porto Moniz** (*see pp122–3*).

4 The north coast road

This road was an astonishing feat of engineering particularly as you realise that the work was carried out by hand by men suspended from the cliffs in wicker baskets. It took 16 years to build the ledges and tunnels carved out of the cliff faces. Remnants of the single-track road remain but can only be

travelled in an east–west direction.
Take the road marked ER101 Antiga to
the right of every tunnel entrance. One
section to **Ribeira Funda** is worth
taking despite its being a dead end just
to experience driving up the spiral
tunnel to the village perched between
two cliffs.

Porto Moniz (*see pp122–3*) has a good
fish restaurant and is known for its
natural swimming pools in the lava rock.
*Take the ER101 out of the village looking
down on the patchwork of tiny fields
hedged in by bracken. Continue about
4km (2½ miles) to the ER110 on the left,
by a cattle market.*

5 Paúl da Serra

This road takes you high above one of
Madeira's deepest ravines and across the
bleak moorland plateau of **Paúl da
Serra**. At times the road is raised above

the moorland because of the high risk
of flooding. If you have time, stop at
where the road forks to the left
signposted **Rabaçal** (*see p124*).
This is where the *levada* walk to
Risco Waterfall (*see pp130–31*) starts.
From here you can also walk to the
Lagoa das 25 Fontes.

6 From Rabaçal

Continue on the ER110 across the Paúl
da Serra along the only significant
stretch of straight road in Madeira to
Boca da Encumeada. You will pass a
forest of wind turbines before
descending through a series of hairpin
bends and tunnels with stunning views
down on perched villages and terraced
smallholdings.
*Take the route you took earlier to return
to Funchal with the option of taking the
expressway from Ribeira Brava.*

The picturesque village of Câmara de Lobos

Walk: Risco Waterfall

Risco Waterfall is one of the most scenic spots on Madeira and the short walk to the fall is well worth doing as a break from the tour of western Madeira.

Allow 1 hour from Rabaçal or 3½ hours if walking from the car park on the ER110. The directions here are from Rabaçal.

Start at Rabaçal. Do not be put off by the information board in the car park beside the ER110 which states the walk takes 3½ hours. This is the time taken for the return trip from the car park. You cannot now drive to Rabaçal but have to walk or take the regular minibus service (9.30am–7.30pm. Admission charge) down the narrow winding road.

Rabaçal

A short way down the road, you will cross a river bed, albeit a very shallow one. This is the **Ribeira do Alecrim** (meaning 'Rosemary River'), named after the rosemary that grows along its pretty banks and pools.

After 2km (1¼ miles) you will come to a small car park, next to a government rest house, which has picnic tables and a terrace. This is Rabaçal, a delightful spot: the name means 'virgin', 'primeval' or 'unspoilt', and looking out from the terrace over the green valley below it is not difficult to see why it has been given this name.

Levada do Risco

From the car park, follow the dirt track that leads downhill: it is on the right as you face the rest house. Very soon this will bring you down to the **Levada do Risco**, which follows the valley side at a height of 1,030m (3,380ft).

The woodland on both sides of the *levada* is magical: the gnarled trees are hung with great hanks of lime green lichen, and wild goats feed among the many tumbled boulders that lie scattered across the hillside. The undergrowth consists of tree heath (*Erica arborea*).

The Levada do Risco passes under the **Risco Waterfall**, about a 30-minute walk from the car park. Although the area is beautiful, it can be dangerous: that lovely green lichen that you were admiring at the beginning of the walk is increasingly wet and slippery the closer you get to the Risco Waterfall.

Levada das 25 Fontes

Following the path, you will pass a signposted junction – the way left leads downhill, and then right to the spot known as **Vinte e Cinco Fontes** (25 Springs). You can return later, if you wish, and take this path, which leads, after about an hour, to a pool into which tumble numerous little waterfalls.

The route to Risco continues straight ahead, and, as you pass along the path, sweeping views open up on the left, looking down the green and unspoilt valley of the Ribeira Grande.

Risco Waterfall

The sound of the waterfall will greet you before you see it. Just before the fall, the path divides: keep to the right, climbing up the concrete wall of the *levada* – and ignore the wider path to the left, which leads a short way downhill to a reservoir and then stops. Rounding a corner, you will see the fall, its waters cascading from a height of 100m (330ft).

Don't be tempted to walk behind the fall; the ground and walls are extremely slippery and hazardous. If it is a warm day and you are overheated from the walk, simply relax and enjoy a close view of the fall while the mist soaks and cools you. You will dry off on the walk back to Rabaçal. For those accustomed to strenuous walks and climbs it will be tempting to continue, but, again, heed the warning signs along the trail and do not walk beyond the fall.

Walk: Risco Waterfall

The view from the Levada do Risco; high rainfall and humidity encourage the lush valley greenery and the growth of different types of lichen and moss

Porto Santo

The small island of Porto Santo is a complete contrast to Madeira. Where Madeira is lush and green, Porto Santo is arid and brown. On Madeira, the coastline is dominated by towering cliffs, while the 9km (5½ miles) of sandy beach is the main coastal feature of Porto Santo. Deep valleys with steep slopes characterise the landscapes of Madeira but on Porto Santo, the few mountains are separated by a plain.

Porto Santo has sun, sea and sand and as such attracts Madeirans for their holidays. The island's population of around 5,000 increases to 25,000 in August so is best avoided during this period, when it is crowded and prices are at their highest.

All the hotels and campsite are built along the strip of land behind the beach. In recent years the pace of this development has increased with several new hotels. Some, like the Pestana Porto Santo, a five-star luxury resort, are a good distance from Vila Baleira and as transport links are not keeping pace with the development of hotels and timeshares, this can be a bit of an issue if you want to visit other parts of the island.

Sheer remoteness has ensured that Porto Santo's beach remains relatively undeveloped and unspoilt, a paradise for those who enjoy idle sunbathing or more active watersports, such as windsurfing.

Getting there

There are several flights a day between Madeira's main airport and Porto Santo. The 37km (23-mile) journey takes a mere 15 minutes. The fare is quite expensive but flights are often fully booked in the summer season, so it is advisable to book in advance through **TAP** (Air Portugal) (*Avenida das Comunidades Madeirenses 10. Tel: (291) 239211*), or through a travel agent.

By sea, the journey is on a luxury cruise liner equipped with cinemas, restaurants and game rooms; it takes two and a half hours depending on the weather. If the sea is rough, people prone to seasickness should consider flying. Car ferries leave Funchal's marina at 8am and return by 9pm. Bookings can be made through any travel agent or directly with the cruise line office on the marina, **Porto Santo Line** (*tel: (291) 210300*).

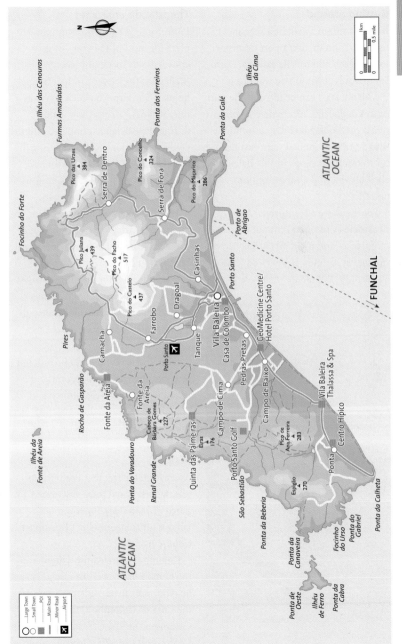

Getting around

It is a 20-minute walk or a very short taxi ride from the ferry port or airport to the beach and to **Vila Baleira**, Porto Santo's only town. If you want to tour the island, taxis can be hired at the port or in Vila Baleira. Alternatively, you can rent a car, book a boat trip around the island or join a guided tour; just head for the seafront shops in Vila Baleira and you will find all these options on offer.

For the more adventurous, **Auto Acessórios Colombo** rent out bicycles, motorbikes and quad bikes. They are situated at Avenida H Vieira de Castro 64 (*tel: (291) 984438*).

Porto Santo's seemingly endless ribbon of sand

The island's character

Porto Santo is a pretty uncomplicated place for most of the year – it gets crowded only in August when Madeirans flock over for their annual holiday. The airport, which serves as a reserve NATO airbase, saw action during the Falklands campaign and the Gulf War, but for most of the time the islanders enjoy a peaceful existence, tending tiny plots where figs, melons, grapes and pumpkins are grown.

Wind turbines built on the island to generate electricity are obvious but a closer look at the landscape will reveal several traditional windmills with canvas sails used for grinding corn. At least one of these is still in working order. Donkeys are used for transport, and the upland areas are grazed by cattle and sheep.

Overall, the island looks brown and arid, but there are springs on the island feeding the irrigation system, and one of them produces bottled mineral water.

History

Apart from the fact that Porto Santo was the first island to be 'discovered' by Zarco in 1418 (*see p10*), it is more famous for someone else: Christopher Columbus.

Columbus married the daughter of the island's first governor (*see p17*) and he reportedly lived on Porto Santo at the **Casa de Colombo** (House of Columbus) at Rua Cristovão Colombo 12 (*tel: (291) 983405. Open: Tue–Sat*

10am–5.30pm, Sun 10am–1pm. Admission charge). The museum has been restored and is made up of a number of rooms of artefacts connected with Columbus and the island's history. There are portraits of Columbus with scenes depicting some of his many adventures. You can view maps of his journeys and models of several of his boats.

A large room off the courtyard contains two sunken grain stores and treasures recovered from the *Carrock*, a Dutch boat owned by the East India Company that sank off the coast of Porto Santo in 1724 while en route to Jakarta. In the museum are Spanish and Dutch coins and silver ingots. Most of the ship's cargo was salvaged by an Englishman, John Lethbridge, in 1726; the rest was recovered in 1974 and donated to the museum.

Remoteness guarantees an unspoilt beach

Touring Porto Santo

Tours of Porto Santo normally take in one or both of the island's volcanic cones; one is the **Pico do Castelo** (Castle Peak), so called because it was once fortified as a defence against pirates; the other is **Pico do Facho** (Torch Peak), the island's highest point (517m/1,696ft), where sentries once lit warning beacons if pirates were sighted. There are wonderful views from both hilltops, sometimes as far as Madeira.

Fonte da Areia (Sand Spring) is where the island's mineral water is bottled, the natural spring rising out of the sandstone which has been much eroded by the wind and waves.

Serra de Dentro is a picturesque uninhabited village, where sheep now graze the abandoned terraces.

Staying on

On an island that is so arid, there is an oasis of luxuriant vegetation, **Quinta das Palmeiras**. It is the result of one man's dream and hard work. Carlos Alfonso designed and built the garden and had to transport in every drop of water by truck. The garden is full of plants and flowers including the ubiquitous hibiscus, roses, red hot pokers and angel's trumpets. Flying free among all this vegetation is a huge variety of birds including parrots and doves (*Sítio dos Linhares. Tel: (291) 983625. Open: daily 10am–1pm & 3–5pm. Admission charge*).

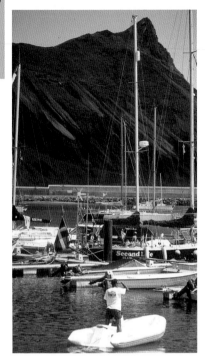

Volcanic peaks tower over Porto Santo's yachting marina

Sport and leisure

Activities popular on the island include cycling or quad biking, diving on the wreck of the *Madeirense*, and all manner of watersports. Although the island lacks the mountainous nature of Madeira there are several marked and maintained walking routes including at least one *levada* walk.

Golf

The island's 18-hole par 72 golf course stretches from just behind the dunes on one side of the island to the dramatic basalt cliffs on the other. It was designed by former world champion Severiano Ballesteros and great care was taken to minimise the impact on the environment. There is also a nine-hole course of par 3 pitch and putt holes and a driving range.
Porto Santo Golf, Sítio das Marinhas. Tel: (291) 983778. www.portosantogolfe.com

Horse riding

The wide open spaces and the beach make the island ideal for horse riding. The **Centro Hípico do Porto Santo** organises pony trekking and lessons of varying degrees of difficulty (*Sítio da Ponta. Tel: (291) 983258*).

Spa and health centres

The people of Porto Santo have claimed for years that the sand on their beach has healing properties, especially for orthopaedic and rheumatic disorders. Visitors to the island would bury themselves in the warm sand of the beach because of these supposed health benefits. A local geologist and Oslo University conducted a study that backed this up and showed that the sand is rich in several beneficial minerals including magnesium, iodine and strontium that are good for treating inflammatory problems and some skin diseases such as psoriasis. Drawing on these therapeutic properties, the **GeoMedicine Centre** (*Campo de Baixo. Tel: (291) 980140. www.hotelportosanto.com*), as part of the Hotel Porto Santo, opened in 2008 and has its roots buried firmly in the sand (quite literally). Their unique Hot Sand Therapy has been clinically proven to help in the treatment of rheumatism and osteoarthritis and to speed recovery after injury.

The island's only thalassotherapy centre, the **Vila Baleira Thalassa and Spa** (*Sítio do Cabeço da Ponta. Tel: (291) 980800. www.vilabaleira.com*), is part of, but independent from, the Hotel Vila Baleira. They offer a variety of sea water treatments and massages alongside beauty treatments.

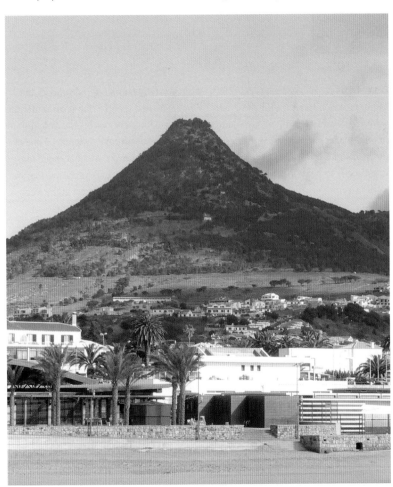

Vila Baleira with Pico do Castelo rising above it

Getting away from it all

It is not difficult to get away from it all on Madeira either on land or at sea, and you are never far from civilisation when you want to return. Indeed, the attraction of Madeira is that you can get away from it all and have the luxury and service at the end of the day.

Boat trips

Madeira is rich territory for those who want to get away from it all; an island of wild places and endless meandering footpaths (*see pp140–41*). Another way to escape is to head for the sea; by joining a mini cruise you can see the island's towering cliffs from a different perspective, and returning to Funchal harbour you will retrace the sea route taken by all visitors to Madeira in the past, before the first commercial aeroplane services began in 1964.

The best half-day excursions by boat take you along the island's southern coast, either eastwards to **Baía da Abra** (*see map p81*) or westwards to **Ponta do Sol**, passing the foot of **Cabo Girão**, one of the world's highest sea cliffs (*see map p119*). Some operators anchor off the island for a while so that you can swim: the waters are very clean and the sea temperature rarely falls below 18°C (64°F) even in December and January. Evening excursions are timed to make the most of the sunset.

Most operators use motorboats, but you can also spend a day at sea under sail on the 20m (66ft) yacht *Albatroz*, built in 1939 and beautifully restored, or one of several catamarans. All boat excursions depart from Funchal's yacht marina, and you can book either direct at the marina offices or through travel agents.

The Ilhas Desertas

For the ultimate away-from-it-all experience you can join one of the occasional boat trips that go to the Ilhas Desertas, the three flat islands 20km (12½ miles) to the southeast of Funchal (*see map p7*). The largest of the islands, **Deserta Grande**, is a long, narrow, 12km-by-1km (7½ mile-by-⅔ mile) plateau of volcanic rock rising to a height of 479m (1,572ft).

The island is arid and the soil is too thin to support crops, though it is home to the very rare, big wolf spider (*Lycosa ingens*), which is black, ferocious and so poisonous that its bite can cause death to humans. All attempts to inhabit Deserta Grande have been short-lived.

However, there is a biological observatory on the island manned by naturalists. Their job is to monitor and protect the wildlife, notably a small colony of monk seals. The seals were once numerous, but raids by Madeiran fishermen resulted in mass slaughter and their near extinction: the fishermen regarded the fish-eating seals as a threat to their livelihood.

The fishermen also killed half the island's bird population in another raid in 1976. To prevent further bloodshed, the island was declared a nature reserve in 1990.

Visitors can visit the island only with a special permit granted exclusively to people engaged in legitimate research projects. You can, however, sail to the islands to watch the seals, and you may also catch sight of dolphins and turtles.

There are also many seabirds to be seen around the islands, including Cory's, Manx and the Madeiran little shearwater, plus Bulwer's soft-plumaged and Madeiran petrels. A visit to Funchal's Municipal Museum (*see pp50–51*) will help you identify all of these.

Gaviao, based in Funchal's marina, runs boat trips to the Ilhas Desertas every Thursday (weather permitting) departing at 10am and returning at 6.30pm (*tel: (291) 241124 for details*). Alternatively, you could try **Ventura do Mar**, who run bird- and dolphin-watching trips (*tel: (291) 280033. www.venturadomar.com*).

Deep-sea fishing

Big fish abound in the deep waters off Madeira, and regular excursions depart from Funchal's marina in search of marlin, tuna, swordfish and shark. Marlin over 453kg (1000lb) are regularly caught, mostly on a tag-and-release scheme.

Trips can be arranged through travel agents, or contact Madeira Big Game Fishing (tel: (291) 227169. www.madeiragamefish.com).

Undersea exploration

If you have never been diving before in your life, Madeira is a great place to have a go, with several schools catering for absolute beginners (*see p140*). The clear blue seas round Madeira's southern coast are rich in underwater caves where you can marvel at the variety of the vegetation and the agility of the multicoloured fish.

Cabo Girão, among the highest cliffs in Europe

Sea bream, mullet and sea perch are quite common, as are squid and octopus, but the real gems of the underwater world are the sea anemone that cling to the black basalt rocks of the seabed, the coral-coloured scorpion fish, and the teeming shoals of tiny fish whose iridescent stripes flash in the gloom as they twist and turn.

There are several diving centres on Madeira and Porto Santo.

Scorpio Divers (*Complexo do Lido, Funchal. Tel: (291) 766977*) takes on everyone, from absolute beginners to experienced divers, and is a British-run sub-aqua club with certified instructors, based in Funchal's Hotel Zone.

Atalaia, based in Caniço, offers equipment hire and courses (*tel: (291) 934330*). So does **Tubarão Madeira** at the Pestana Palms Hotel in Funchal (*tel: 96 5011126*).

Hiking

There were very few roads on Madeira until the 1960s – instead, a complex network of footpaths criss-crossed the island, linking up with the equally extensive system of pathways running alongside the island's *levadas*, or irrigation canals (*see pp142–3*). These footpaths make Madeira a wonderful place for long-distance walking, with all the attractions of panoramic views, waterfalls, scented woodlands, abundant flora and arresting geological formations. A good map is essential.

Well worth the effort: the view from Balcões

Beginners

Although Madeira's climate is balmy – it can get rather warm when walking the uphill and downhill footpaths – be sure to wear light clothing, absorbent socks and sturdy boots. Four walks along well-trodden footpaths are detailed in this guide (*see pp76–7, 88–9, 106–7 & 130–31*). To get the most pleasure out of *levada* walking you might consider joining guided walks. Walks with specialists such as **Strawberry World** (Lido Tours) (*Centro Comercial Monumental Lido, Estrada Monumental, Funchal. Tel: (291) 762429. www.lido-tours.com*) are led by knowledgeable mountain guides. Tours can be booked directly with the company, or through travel agents or the tourist office in Funchal.

Experienced walkers

The bible for serious walkers on Madeira is John and Pat Underwood's

Landscapes of Madeira, which is sold in just about every newsagents and souvenir shop on the island. Opinions differ, naturally enough, on which walks are the very best, but if you are short of time, most people agree that the following three are difficult to beat for variety and scenic value:

• Pico do Arieiro to Pico Ruivo (*the first part of this route is covered on pp106–7*)

• Rabaçal to the waterfall at Risco and Vinte e Cinco Fontes (*part covered on pp130–31*)

• Queimadas to the Caldeirão do Inferno.

Footwear and clothing

Not all of Madeira is easy for walking; there are many treacherous mountain paths, particularly with the *levadas*. It is important to bring the proper footwear; you will need mountain boots, particularly for walking/hiking the *levadas*. They should be waterproof and have a good grip to prevent slipping on wet rocks, mossy paths and scree slopes. Also bring lightweight clothing, sunblock, a waterproof anorak and a hat. Every year many unprepared visitors suffer serious injuries, some requiring hospitalisation, because they trip or slip walking the mountainous regions of Madeira.

Planning and precautions

Nothing in the world is ever perfect, and the big drawback for walkers on Madeira is the cost and time involved in getting to and from the start and end points of your walk. Some people get round this by camping or sleeping out under the stars, but by adopting this approach you miss one of Madeira's big attractions: the chance to walk all day among mountain peaks and then retire at night not to some sweaty alpine hut, but to a comfortable hotel with a shower and a good restaurant.

Buses offer a cheap and reliable way of getting to and from your walk, but for optimum freedom it is best to hire a car or use a taxi. If you team up with other walkers you can share the cost between four or five – it is, in any case, advisable not to go walking on your own in case you have an accident.

If you do go out alone, be sure to tell someone where you are going and what time you can be expected back so that the alarm can be raised if you fail to return.

Many beautiful parts of the island are accessible only on foot

Levadas

The *levadas* of Madeira are a unique and endearing feature of the island, forming an astonishing network of irrigation canals, some 2,150km (1,336 miles) in total length. The earliest canals date right back to the colonisation of the island in the 15th and 16th centuries, though most were dug, entirely by hand, in the early part of the 20th century.

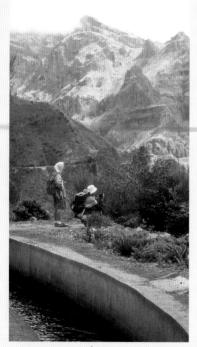

A *levada* winding round a mountainside

The purpose of *levadas* is to distribute water from those parts of the island that have plenty – notably the north side, where average annual rainfall tops 2m (6^1/2ft) – to the dry areas, such as the sunny south where the economically important grape and banana crops are grown.

The *levadas* are fed both by natural springs and by reservoirs – giant storage tanks built up in the mountains. Water from the outfalls is first put to work driving the turbines of the island's electricity-generating power stations.

Maintaining the *levadas* is an important job, entrusted to the *levadeiro*, who patrols his allotted length of *levada* to keep the waters flowing, clear up landslips and unblock grilles designed to filter out leaves and debris. He is also responsible for operating the complex system of sluices and watergates which divert water to the individual properties bordering the *levada* according to a carefully worked-out schedule.

To do this, the *levadeiro* needs access to the water channels – hence the footpaths that run alongside, built for purely functional reasons but coincidentally offering a paradise for

Levadas penetrate where no roads go

walkers. They penetrate the most inaccessible depths of the island, running up the sides of deep ravines and carefully terraced valleys, always following the contours of the terrain so that, once you are on the path, there is no strenuous climbing.

The path they weave is always varied, sometimes passing through rock-cut tunnels, at other times through ancient woodland hung with moss and lichens, and sometimes alongside sunny cherry orchards or market gardens. Best of all, they take you to places where the modern world has yet to penetrate, far from the sound of traffic, but full of the sounds of birds and gently running water.

Shopping

Part of the pleasure of shopping on Madeira is watching souvenirs being made before you buy them. Factories producing both embroidery and wickerwork put on demonstrations, and they don't make you feel obliged to buy anything. In fact, Madeiran shopkeepers do not go in for high-pressure sales techniques at all and the welcome absence of hassle only adds to the pleasure of browsing through Funchal's many shops.

The best shops are located in the streets immediately north and south of the cathedral. If you are exploring this area, don't forget to look down the little side alleys, as well as the main streets, where some of the most characterful shops are tucked away.

Practical details

Madeira is a shoppers' and bargain hunters' paradise. There are plenty of shopping centres located in Funchal, and they are open from 10am to 10pm daily (except Sundays in some places).

If you crave a mall atmosphere, then head to **Madeira Shopping**, the largest shopping centre on the island, in the Santa Quitéria section of Funchal. Here you will find, under one roof, 83 shops that sell everything from designer clothes to electrical goods, 7 cinemas, 20 restaurants (some with terraces offering a view of the sea) and what Madeirans call Microlândia –

bowling, virtual reality machines and mini golf.

Between the Avenida do Mar and the Avenida do Infante is the smaller **Marina Shopping**, which caters for cruise passengers. There are three floors of shops selling everything from chic clothing and accessories to books, antiques and surfing gear. The most recent shopping centre is the centrally located **Dolce Vita**. Part of a hotel and spa complex, it is an airy building with plenty of glass and space with over 70 shops, cafés and bars and a health complex. Funchal's most established shopping streets are near the marina and the Avenida Arriaga to Avenida Zarco and up to Rua Dr Fernão Ornelas and any avenue in between. Take a city map and go exploring to find that something special to take home. Don't just shop the main avenues; the narrow back streets have some interesting shops also. There are many shops offering the two most popular souvenir items: wicker and embroidery.

What to buy and where

Antiques

Furniture, mirrors, copper pans, old *azulejos* (tiles), or even hand-carved crib figures – all these are worth looking out for in the little cluster of antique shops opposite São Pedro church.

Bolo de mel

If you get hooked on Madeira's solid and filling 'honey cake', you can buy supplies to take home at numerous *pastelarias*, or baker's shops, such as the one at Rua da Carreira 75. The cake will keep for many months but traditionally a new batch is made on 8 December ready for the Christmas festivities, and any old cake is eaten up on the same day.

Books

If you run out of books to read by the hotel pool, you can buy all the latest English bestsellers at the **Patio Bookshop**, Rua da Carreira 43. The shop also sells guidebooks and usually has a small stock of very interesting illustrated antiquarian guides to Madeira; these make an unusual souvenir and bring back a sense of the island's recent British 'colonial' past.

Boots

You can buy traditional Madeiran leather boots with a turned-down top at roadside stalls and souvenir shops all over Madeira. If you want to see how they are made, visit **Gonçalves & Silva**'s workshop at Rua do Portão de São Tiago 22, in the Zona Velha (Old Town).

Embroidery

Handmade embroidery (*bordados*) is one of the island's most important exports. The art of embroidery was introduced to Madeira by Elizabeth Phelps, daughter of a British wine shipper, during the 1850s, as a means of supplementing the islanders' meagre incomes. The samples Miss Phelps took to London were warmly received, and by 1862 there were 1,000 women employed in the business.

Today, that number has grown to 20,000 embroiderers, but this remains a cottage-based industry.

Genuine handmade embroidery always carries a lead tag fixed to one corner as a guarantee of quality awarded by the island's handicraft institute, IBTAM (*see p43*). In any case, you will soon learn to recognise the genuine article, which is very elegant but also rather expensive, being a labour-intensive product.

Some of the big exporters welcome visitors to their factory showrooms, where you can watch the pattern printing processes and the final finishing of garments and table linen. One of the best factories to visit is **Patricio & Gouveia**, at Rua do Visconde de Anadia 34.

Flowers

Shopping for flowers in the Mercado dos Lavradores, or Workers' Market (*see p47*), can be great fun, but it is best to buy from a florist if you want your flowers packed in special boxes for travelling.

Popular, long-lasting Madeiran flowers include orchids (in season from late November to May), *strelitzias* (birds of paradise) and anthuriums (flamingo flowers), the last two available all year. You can also take home bulbs, seeds and baby orchid plants, provided that there is no soil with them.

Food

Gourmets will enjoy browsing in little delicatessens such as the one at Rua do Carmo 11. Best buys are Portuguese olive oil, fresh walnuts in season and *lapas escabeche*, limpets preserved in brine and vinegar, an unusual ingredient for a seafood salad or pasta sauce.

Hats

Bobble hats with earflaps, as worn by Madeiran farmers to keep off the rain, or straw boaters, as worn by the Monte toboggan drivers, can always be bought from roadside stalls – or try **Salão Londrino** (*Rua dos Ferreiros 128, Funchal*).

Knitwear

Knitted cotton sweaters and cardigans are another bargain. They are bought at wayside stalls by visitors who discover how much colder it can be in Madeira's mountains.

Leather

Shoes, bags, belts and clothing, mostly imported from the Portuguese

Knitwear comes in all colours and designs

mainland, are very good value, especially if you compare prices in Madeira with the fashion shops of northern Europe. To see a good range of stock visit **Pele** (*Rua dos Murcas 26*) or **Arte Couro** (*Rua da Alfândega 15*).

For really upmarket but still affordable products, the best stockists are: **Charles** (*Largo do Chafariz 22*); **Yaya** (*Rua Câmara Pestana 3*); **Godiva** (*Avenida Arriaga 11–13*); **Chloé** (*Largo do Phelps 12*).

Pottery, porcelain, glass and home furnishings

Casa Turística, in Rua do Conselheiro José Silvestre Ribeiro, is a must for all kinds of souvenirs, but especially for ceramics – whether you want just a cachepot for your potted plants or a full dinner service. The shop is laid out like a cross between a private mansion and a museum, with antiques and oil paintings hung beneath ornate plastered ceilings and forming a background for excellent displays.

Other good stores selling contemporary Portuguese designs in crafts such as textiles, pottery, furniture or glass include **Cayres** (*Rua Dr Fernão Ornelas 56*), and **Galeria das Louças** (*Rua do Sabão*).

Souvenirs

Among the less expensive are dolls in Madeiran costume, musical instruments such as the *brinquinho*, DVDs and videotapes of the island and miniature bottles of island liqueurs. **Madeira Sun** (*Avenida Zarco 4*), sells all the typical souvenirs, as does the **Bazar Monte Carlo** (*Rua dos Murcas 19*), and **Rosa d'Ouro** (*Rua de António José d'Almeida*).

Tapestry

The craft of sewing pictures on canvas was introduced to Madeira by the German artist Herbert Kiekeben in 1938. The **Kiekeben** shop, at Rua da Carreira 194, sells wall hangings, chair covers, handbags and carpets, and you can buy do-it-yourself tapestry kits in **Madeira Sun** (*Avenida Zarco 4*).

Wickerwork

The heart of wicker production is at Camacha (*see pp80–81*), and although some wickerwork may be purchased

throughout the island it is to this village that the visitor should head for the complete range of products and for demonstrations by craftsmen at work. However, if Camacha is not on your itinerary, there is a well-stocked shop in Funchal (*Rua da Carreira 102*).

Wines and liqueurs

Many Madeiran souvenir shops sell miniatures and full bottles of non-vintage Madeira, but serious wine lovers should visit Funchal's various wine lodges. The best known is the **Adegas de São Francisco** (*see pp30 & 34–5*), which has a tasting bar and a well-stocked shop, but you should also visit **D'Oliveiras**, at Rua dos Ferreiros 107, an old wine lodge full of dark timbers and delicious smells, or its near neighbour, **Henriques & Henriques** (*Rua dos Ferreiros 125*), whose central courtyard is shaded by rampant vines.

Flowers for sale in Funchal

Entertainment

Nightlife and entertainment on Madeira revolves around the older crowd, as traditionally the majority of tourists fall into that age group. However, there is a shift towards a younger, more adventurous visitor and the nightlife, particularly in the capital, Funchal, is beginning to reflect this with a lot more bars and clubs.

Shows and themed entertainment

Many of the four- and five-star hotels in the Hotel Zone in Funchal offer weekly programmes with themed evenings opened to the public. Mostly these are Madeiran folklore evenings combined with a typical Madeiran dinner. The **Royal Savoy** (*Rua Carvalho Araújo. Tel: (291) 775936*) and **Four Views Hotel Monumental Lido** (*Estrada Monumental 284. Tel: (291) 724000*) both put on regular Madeiran evenings.

You will also find regular folk evenings in the **Café Relógio** Restaurant in Camacha (*Tel: (291) 922777*).

Pestana Carlton Park Resort and Casino Funchal

The Pestana Carlton Park Resort & Casino offers four shows a week that feature songs and routines from popular Broadway musicals. There's also an Oldies show with hits from the 1960s up to the present and, on Sundays, a Paris revue featuring the cancan.

Prices include a four-course dinner, as well as free entrance after the shows to the casino and the Copa Cabana disco. *Rua da Imperatriz Dona Amélia. Tel: (291) 209100.*

Casino
The Madeira Casino

Located in the grounds of the Carlton Park Hotel, the Casino da Madeira offers visitors the opportunity to try their luck playing roulette, blackjack or the slot machines.

The casino is open Sunday to Thursday 3pm–3am and Friday and Saturday 4pm–4am for people over 21 years of age. You will have to show your passport to gain entry, and men are expected to wear a jacket and tie. *Carlton Park Resort and Casino. Tel: (291) 209100. Admission charge.*

Cinema

Popular films are shown in the original language (usually English), with

Portuguese subtitles at several cinemas in Funchal (times are published daily in the free *Notícias da Madeira* newspaper, available at hotels).

More serious films are shown at the Avenida Arriaga, opposite the Tourist Information Office.

Cultural events

Funchal

The **Teatro Municipal** (*Avenida Arriaga. Tel: (291) 226371*) is the venue for classical concerts, theatre and opera performed by local and international artists. There are often classical concerts in the English Church and the cathedral. The Madeira Mandolin Orchestra give weekly concerts in the English Church (*see pp42–3*) that are well worth attending.

The Madeira Cultural Affairs Department (DRAC) publish a monthly listing of events across Madeira in its widely available newsletter Cultural Agenda (also downloadable from *www.madeiratourism.org*).

Porto Santo

The **Cultural and Congress Centre** (*Rua Dr Nuno Silvestre Teixeira, Largo do Pelourinho. Tel: (291) 980600*) is the venue for concerts and other cultural performances. There is also a cinema in Vila Baleira where some of the best films are shown, usually in English with Portuguese subtitles.

Madeira even has a casino, if you feel so inclined

Bars, clubs and discotheques

Funchal

The most popular are given below:

Bar Number 2 Known for its cocktails using *poncha*, the traditional Madeiran rum, and trendy nightlife. It also has a sister bar of the same name in Câmara de Lobos. *Promenade do Lido. Tel: (291) 771635. Open: daily 10am–4am.*

Café do Teatro Located in central Funchal in front of the Municipal Garden, this is a compulsory stop on the Madeiran nightlife scene. Also invites DJs to play music. *Avenida Arriaga. Tel: (291) 759959. Open: daily 9am–4am.*

Copa Cabana is in the basement of the Madeira Casino, and often has live entertainment. *Casino da Madeira, Avenida do Infante. Tel: (291) 233111. Open: daily midnight–4am.*

O Farol A popular disco for those who like the music of the 70s, 80s and 90s. *Madeira Carlton. Tel: (291) 231031. Open: Fri–Sat 11pm–6am.*

FX Bar A bar with a spacious outdoor area. *Avenida do Mar. Tel: (965) 077875. Open: daily 9am–4am.*

Gloria Latina Noteworthy for its colourful Samba shows with Brazilian dancers. A great place if you like Latin rhythms. *Rua da Imperatriz Dona Amélia 68. Tel: (291) 282266.*

The Jam This nightclub features the music of the 70s, 80s and 90s. *Avenida Sá Carneiro 60. Tel: (291) 234800. Open: Wed–Sun midnight–6am.*

O Molhe Located on top of the remains of an old fort incorporated into the harbour wall, this has a dancefloor enclosed by glass so that you can enjoy beautiful views of Funchal, and a bar with a big esplanade where you can sip your drink al fresco and listen to the music at the same time. *Forte de Nossa Senhora da Conceição. Tel: (915) 193034. Open: Fri–Sat midnight–6am.*

Vespas A place for the young, the hip and the trendy, Vespas is the largest nightclub in Madeira and also stays open later than any other venue. For this reason, it is one of the last places on the nightlife circuit and attracts a large crowd of youngsters who really do not want to stop partying. *Avenida Sá Carneiro 60. Tel: (291) 231202. Open: Wed–Sun midnight–6am.*

Beyond Funchal

Bar Number 2 A trendy new bar where *poncha*, the traditional rum of Madeira, is served with a variety of fruit juices in new and experimental ways. *1 Largo Poço, Câmara de Lobos. Tel: (291) 942554. Open: daily 10am–4am.*

La Barca Recently refurbished and thoroughly modernised, this waterfront disco is considered by the locals to be the best outside of Funchal. *Praceta 25 de Abril, Machico. Tel: (291) 965330. Open: daily 10pm–6am.*

Farol Verde A popular bar in Câmara de Lobos, not least because it serves 'Nikitas', a concoction of beer, wine and vanilla ice cream served in a pint glass. *Câmara de Lobos. Tel: (291) 942303. Open: daily 10am–4am.*

Paparazzi A recently refurbished and modern discotheque where you are more likely to meet locals than tourists. *Praceta 25 de Abril, Machico. Tel: (291) 965387.*

Pub Santa Maria Features live music and karaoke. *Sítio do Rosário 75, Santa Cruz. Tel: (291) 523877. Open: daily midnight–4am.*

Porto Santo

Nightlife on Porto Santo is very low-key, with only the larger hotels providing any shows. However, there are a surprising number of bars and restaurants in Vila Baleira where you can mix with the locals and sample the atmosphere. During August the nightlife scene hots up somewhat with the arrival of the hip crowd from Funchal. Clubs such as **Challenger** (*Rua D. Esteva de Alencastre. Tel: (962) 879177*) in the new dockside developement O Penedo do Sono attract top-class DJs.

Fado

It is difficult to account for the enormous popularity of *fado* (meaning 'fate'), the plaintive Portuguese music and song that tells of tragic events, dark destinies and lost loves, yet popular it is, and there are plenty of opportunities to wallow in an evening of soulful fatalism. Madeirans highly rate performances at:

Arsenio's Restaurant
Rua de Santa Maria 169. Tel: (291) 224007. Open: daily noon–2am.

Marcelino
Travessa da Torre 22A, Zona Velha (Old Town). Tel: (291) 230834. Open: daily 10.30pm–4am.

O Pitéu Bar and Restaurant
Rua da Carreira 182A. Tel: (291) 220819. Open: Tue & Fri–Sat.

Some restaurants offer *fado* performances

Music and dance

Madeira's traditional music and dance make light of the heavy burdens of work and slavery. In one very distinctive dance the participants turn in slow circles with their heads bowed, taking short steps as if their feet were chained together. It is called the Dance of Ponta do Sol, named after the area where Moorish and African slaves were kept during the early days of the island's colonisation. Similar in style are the Carrier's Dance, representing heavily laden peasants jogging along the island's footpaths beneath stacks of sugar cane or baskets loaded with bananas, and the Heavy Dance, in which the regular rhythmic stamping is said to reflect the custom of crushing grapes with bare feet to make Madeira wine.

Madeiran song is more light-hearted and tells of courtship, the pleasures of the autumn harvest and the joys of wine. In contrast, the *charamba* is a kind of musical duel, with a lively chorus, in which two singers improvise alternate verses which satirise the other person's

Accordion and *braguinha* accompany songs and dances

The Madeiran song and dance traditions are handed down by each generation

looks, character or reputation, to the amusement of the audience.

Musical accompaniment to both song and dance is provided by the four-stringed *braguinha*, similar to a ukulele, wooden castanets called *castanholas*, and a notched stick called a *raspadeira*, decorated with a carved head and played like a washboard.

Most intriguing of all is the percussive *brinquinho*, a hand-held pole where dolls in Madeiran costume wearing bells and castanets slide up and down in rhythm with the music.

Madeira still has numerous folklore groups who perform at festivals all round the island, dedicated to keeping Madeira's traditions alive. They can also be seen at folklore evenings hosted by Funchal's major hotels and at the **Café Relógio** restaurant in Camacha most evenings (*tel: (291) 922777*).

Children

As a destination, Madeira has, in the past, tended to attract the older visitor rather than young families, so there are fewer facilities for children than you find in other Portuguese resorts. This has been gradually changing, however, and there are a number of new developments specifically aimed at children and families. Children are welcomed warmly wherever you go as Madeirans are very indulgent towards the young.

If your children swim and are old enough to be trusted on their own, they will happily spend hours at the pool. The **Lido Complex** (*see p156*), located in the Hotel Zone on Rua do Gorgulho, is by far the best pool on Madeira. The drawback is that it is packed with people at the weekend, so the best time to take your children is during the week. In contrast, several of the larger hotels have sports facilities that are underused – your children could be encouraged to spend a few hours on the tennis courts or enjoy a few rounds of crazy golf.

Apart from the Lido Complex, there are the natural volcanic rock pools that have been extended and connected together in Porto Moniz and which are very popular with families.

In Santa Cruz the new **Aquaparque** (*Ribeira da Boaventura, Santa Cruz. Tel: (291) 524412. www.aquaparque.com. Open: daily Aug 10am–7pm, Sept–Jul 10am–6pm. Admission charge*) with five toboggan rides, four chutes, two

swimming pools (one reserved for children) and a lazy river will appeal to children of all ages.

Of the museums in Funchal, the **Museu Municipal** (*see pp50–51*) will probably prove the most appealing, both for the stuffed sharks and other monsters of the deep upstairs, and for the live fish, crabs and lobsters in the small downstairs aquarium.

The **Madeira Theme Park** (*see pp108–9*) in Santana with its rides, simulators and multimedia shows provides a great deal of fun for children while being educational at the same time. They cannot help but come away knowing more about Madeira.

The **Volcanism Centre** and the **Grutas de São Vicente** (*see p112*) are another fun museum that children will enjoy. After exploring the caves they can see how the islands of Madeira were formed through a multimedia show.

Another museum with plenty of interactive displays that will appeal to children is the **Madeira Story Centre**. It tells the story of Madeira from its formation to the present day.

Gorgeously coloured tropical birds can be seen at the **Jardim dos Loiros** (*see pp64–5*), and there is a small 'zoo' in the public gardens in Santo da Serra, featuring deer, birds of prey and a kangaroo. Neither of these will absorb your children's attention for very long, however, and those who are attuned to environmental issues may well be repelled by the conditions in which the animals and birds are kept.

Younger children can burn off energy in the small playground in the **Parque de Santa Catarina** (*see pp58–9*), which has swings, climbing frames and plenty of space to run around in, and they will probably find it as much fun to watch the antics of the scurrying wall lizards, or chase the large butterflies with their tissue-paper wings.

Walking by the seafront is another way to spend some time watching the boats coming and going. The marina waters are surprisingly clean and clear and you can watch shoals of silvery fish darting and turning in the sun-warmed waters.

There are numerous boat trips from Funchal harbour but the one that excites children the most is the replica of the **Santa Maria**, the ship that took Columbus on his journey of discovery across the Atlantic in the 15th century. There are daily trips along the coast and, for the adults, romantic twilight cruises (*Marina do Funchal. Tel: (291) 220237. Open: Jun–Sept daily 10.30am– 1.30pm, 3.00–6.00pm & 7.15–8.45pm (plus twilight cruises). Admission charge*).

A ride up to **Monte** (*see pp67–9 & 73*) in the cable car and a thrilling ride down on the toboggan is almost as good as any theme park ride and popular with children.

A trip on Columbus's ship the *Santa Maria* is always a success with children

Sport and leisure

Quite a number of Madeira's visitors come with the idea of getting some gentle exercise and keeping fit, so the better hotels all have pools and tennis courts. The island has three golf courses in spectacular settings, and though it lacks beaches, there is plenty of scope for watersports, including scuba-diving and fishing (see p139).

Hotel facilities

If sports are your priority then it is worth choosing your hotel based on the facilities it offers. Five-star seafront hotels such as the **Hotel Savoy Classic**, **Madeira Palácio**, **Pestana Carlton Madeira**, **Reid's** and the **Pestana Carlton Park Resort and Casino** have tennis courts and swimming pools large enough for serious workouts.

The **Royal Savoy** (*tel: (291) 213000*) has the best seafront complex of all the hotels; there is access to windsurfing, sailing, sea-canoeing, miniature golf and a putting green, along with a fitness centre and tennis courts. The **Pestana Carlton Park Resort and Casino** (*tel: (291) 209100*) offers a high-tech fitness centre, whirlpool and tennis.

Guests are given first priority to the hotels' amenities and using the facilities, but most hotels will admit non-residents for an admission fee. It is worth enquiring whether the hotel will waive the admission fee if you dine there.

The Lido Complex

For serious swimmers and for families with children, the **Lido Complex**, on Rua do Gorgulho, offers a good alternative to hotel facilities. The complex includes an Olympic-size pool, a children's pool, access to the sea from a diving platform, solariums and several cafés and restaurants.

Open daily from 8.30am to 8pm in summer and 8.30am to 7pm in winter, the Lido is well worth visiting during the week, but with 3,000 visitors packed into the complex at weekends, it can seem unbearably overcrowded.

Quinta Magnólia

Madeira's other public facility is the elegant **Quinta Magnólia** (*tel: (291) 764598*) on Rua Dr Pita. Formerly the British Country Club, the Quinta's palm-filled gardens, with public pool, tennis courts, jogging track and playground, offer a quiet oasis in a busy part of Funchal.
Grounds open: daily 8am–9.30pm.

The building now houses the **Biblioteca de Culturas Estrangeiras** (Foreign Culture Library) (*tel: (291) 233164. Open: Mon–Fri 9am–5.30pm*). The library has an excellent supply of international books that anyone can borrow for free.

Football

Madeirans are passionate about football; they claim the game was introduced to Portugal via Madeira. The **Estádio dos Barreiros** stadium, whose concrete bulk looms north of the Hotel Zone, is home to one of Madeira's first division clubs, CS Marítimo, the other being Nacional, who play across town at the **Eng Rui Alves** stadium. Football is a family affair and there is no risk of violence. CS Marítimo's stadium stands high above Funchal, so, as the locals say, if there's not much happening on the field, you can always enjoy the view.

Golf

Madeira has three golf courses, all noted for their magnificent views and picturesque setting. The 27-hole **Santo da Serra** course (*tel: (291) 550100*) is set high at 500m (1,640ft) on a plateau to the east of the island. This is the venue for the Madeira Open tournament, held every January, which attracts many top international players. The 18-hole **Palheiro Golf** (*tel: (291) 790126*) is situated high above Funchal and carved out of the 324ha (800-acre) Quinta do Palheiro estate (*see pp74–5*).

Madeira's newest course, **Porto Santo Golfe**, can be found on the nearby island of Porto Santo (*tel: (291) 983778*).

Horse riding

Contact the **Associação Hípica da Madeira** (*Quinta Vila Alpires, Caminho dos Pretos, São João de Latrão. Tel: (291) 792582). Open: Tue 3–6pm, Wed–Sun 10am–1pm & 3–6pm*). Arrangements can also be made at the **Hotel Estrelícia** (*Caminho Velha da Ajuda. (tel: (291) 706600)*. The **Centro Hípico do Porto Santo** organises riding tours on the island of Porto Santo (*Sítio da Ponta. Tel: (291) 983258*).

The Santo da Serra golf course

Food and drink

Madeira's mild climate allows al fresco dining at any time of the day, all year round. Most restaurants have patios or rooftop terraces. The food is fresh and, for the most part, inexpensive. Dining in the hotels will offer more choices, but it can be pricey. For good value dine in the smaller restaurants and cafés in Funchal, or, better yet, outside the city. You might try marisqueiras – *restaurants specialising in seafood, or* churrascarias, *which serve grilled foods.*

WHAT TO EAT

It may seem that Madeiran menus are deliberately designed to confuse non-Portuguese visitors. Three of the most popular dishes all have very similar names: *espada* (scabbard fish), *espadarte* (swordfish) and *espetada* (beef kebabs). Learn the difference between these three, and you will have the key to eating well during your stay.

Espada

Espada are the rather ugly-looking elongated fish that you will see for sale in the Mercado dos Lavradores (Workers' Market) in Funchal. The name *espada* means 'sword', referring to their long, flat shape. Once cleaned and prepared for cooking they look innocuous enough, but in the market their long snout, vicious teeth and over-large eyes are the stuff of nightmares.

In fact, *espada* are very unusual fish, unique to the waters around Madeira and to certain islands in Japan. They live at very great depths – below 800m

(2,600ft), hence their large eyes, necessary for seeing in the gloom. They are carnivorous, so have razor-sharp teeth, and they rise to 500m (1,640ft) at night to feed, which is when Madeira's fishermen make their catch, using long lines with up to 150 hooks baited with squid. Decompression kills the fish before they reach the surface and their meat is very versatile: in authentic Madeiran restaurants it is likely to be served *com banana* (fried in butter with a slice of banana on top) or *com vinho e garlic* (marinated in wine before being fried in olive oil); in tourist restaurants it is more likely to be served with white wine sauce and prawns.

Espadarte and other fish

Espadarte, or swordfish, is one of several big and meaty fish that you will find on the menu in restaurants specialising in fish and seafood. Others include *pargo* (bream), *salmonete* (red mullet) and *atum* (tuna), usually served grilled with onion sauce and accompanied by *milho frito*, deep-fried cubes of maize flour mixed with cabbage and herbs.

Nearly all fish restaurants serve seafood paella (*arroz de marisco*) because it is such a spectacular dish, garlanded with prawns and decked with all kinds of shellfish, but the dish and its ingredients are imported for the sake of visitors and it is likely to be expensive. If you want to go native, then try *bacalhau à Gomes de Sá* (salt cod casseroled with onions, potatoes, garlic and olives, and garnished with chopped boiled eggs) or *caldeirada*, a tasty fish stew made from fish, potatoes, onions and tomatoes.

Espetada

Espetada consists of chunks of beef, skewered on a stick made from the fresh green wood of the bay tree, which imparts flavour to the meat as it cooks. The meat is rolled in chopped garlic, sea salt and crushed bay leaves, and traditionally the kebabs are grilled over the embers of a fire made from vine prunings, which adds another subtle layer of flavouring. This dish, once reserved for special festivities, such as Christmas and the Feast of the Assumption, is now the staple of Madeiran restaurant menus, where it is often cooked under an electric grill and thus lacks the genuine taste of wood-cooked meat. At some rural restaurants, such as the **Abrigo do Poiso** (*tel: (291) 782269*), located at Poiso (*see pp98–9*) on the road between

Funchal and Faial, you can watch *espetada* being cooked the traditional way, on an open fire, and savour the difference. To accompany the meat, chips and salad are usually served, and in traditional restaurants chunks of *bolo de caco*. This country bread is made from nothing but flour, sweet potatoes and a small amount of yeast and water; allowed to prove for 24 hours, it is then shaped into flat circles and cooked quickly on top of a flat stone heated in the same open fire used to cook the kebabs. The result is a spongy, open-textured bread with a delicious crust.

The Madeiran menu

As soon as you are seated at any good Madeiran café or restaurant table, the

Espada: ugly but delicious

Espetada: traditionally grilled over the aromatic wood of vines or bay trees

waiter is likely to present you with a plate of warm bread dripping with garlic butter. Hoping that the garlic will counterbalance the cholesterol effects of the butter, you can enjoy this deliciously simple food while pondering the menu.

Starters

The most typical Madeiran starters are grilled limpets and tomato soup. With limpets (*lapas*) you risk pushing the cholesterol count even higher, since they are often served in the shell in a puddle of melted garlic butter, but these are the only native Madeiran shellfish – everything else is imported. Far healthier is *sopa de tomate* made from finely chopped onions and tomatoes with a lightly poached egg added to each person's bowl before serving.

Main courses and side dishes

All main courses come with potatoes (boiled with fish, chips with meat) and salad or vegetables, so you do not need to order any side dishes unless you wish. If you do order a side dish, make it clear you want it served at the same time as the main course, otherwise it will be presented on its own, after the starter.

Desserts

Rarely will you be offered much of a choice. Ice cream is ubiquitous, but you may be offered fruit salad – if this is fresh it can be delicious, incorporating the best of the island's tropical varieties, such as papaya, passion fruit, mangoes and custard apples.

Drinks

Coral beer is brewed on Madeira and is a light, refreshing lager with a flowery fragrance. Madeiran table wine is also very drinkable but it is hard to find in Funchal, despite laws requiring bars and restaurants to offer it on their wine lists. Restaurateurs make more money from selling expensive imported wines; if you ask for local wine you are quite likely to be told 'it's not very nice'. In reality, the local wine is light, refreshing, only just fermented, and as much like grape juice in character as wine. Look out for what the locals drink.

Among imported wines, chilled and slightly sparkling *vinho verde* (young or 'green' wine) is a reliable choice to accompany fish, and the robust oaky reds from Dão and Bairrada reveal their rich character when drunk with meat.

Coffee on Madeira is continental in style – you will be served an espresso (*bica* in Portuguese) unless you request otherwise. With it you could try one of Madeira's numerous liqueurs: *maracujá* (made from passion fruit, and said to be an excellent aphrodisiac), *ginja* (made from cherries) and *licor de castanha* (distilled from sweet chestnuts).

Snacks

Madeira's staple lunchtime sandwich is the *prego no prato*, made from country bread spread with garlic butter and enclosing a chunk of grilled steak, a robust and filling energy-reviver served in traditional bars or cafés. Vegetarians have a harder time, but new-style cafés such as **Vivaldi** (*Rua da Figueira Preta 6, just off Rua 31 de Janeiro. Tel: (291) 222028*) are beginning to appear, offering delicatessen-style salads and gourmet sandwiches, plus very good home-made ice cream.

Another staple is *bolo de mel* (honey cake), sold in every *pastelaria* (baker's shop). Traditionally made at Christmas but consumed all year, this dark, fruit-

Grilled limpets in garlic-flavoured butter

filled, spicy cake contains many ingredients – but honey is not one of them; the sweetness comes from the hot molasses added to the cake dough before it is cooked, a legacy of Madeira's ancient sugar-cane industry.

WHERE TO EAT

Wherever you dine ambience and location should count a great deal in your decision. For location there is the Hotel Zone with its well-stocked five-star hotel restaurants, where you will find the largest and priciest choice of international haute cuisine as well as excellent Italian, Chinese and Indian restaurants.

Sugar-cane spirit, drunk with lemon and honey

For atmosphere, go where Madeirans go, the centre, where you will find a plethora of restaurants offering traditional foods such as garlic prawns, grilled tuna and plank steaks.

If you are a seafood fanatic, then the restaurants lining Funchal's yacht marina are the best bet. Here you can select crabs or lobsters live from the tank or choose from a vast range of shellfish or grilled fresh fish – and look out on to magnificent views of the mast-filled marina while you eat.

Further east, many of the pavement cafés of the Zona Velha (Old Town) offer the cheapest prices in Funchal and a festive, youthful atmosphere that is particularly appealing at weekends in summer when some cafés lay on musical entertainment and the party goes on well into the night.

There are no vegetarian restaurants to speak of on the island, and dishes which do not contain meat or fish are hard to come by at most restaurants. Madeira is not the ideal destination for vegetarians.

PRICES

It is easy to eat well and cheaply on Madeira if you eat local food and drink local wines. The prices begin to rise as soon as you go for anything imported. Don't forget, too, that some dishes, especially seafood and fish, are priced according to weight and by the prevailing market price: before you order what may be an expensive out-of-season fish, check with the waiter to get an idea of what a portion will cost.

In most Madeiran restaurants you will not have to order a side dish. The main courses are usually served with fresh salads and chips or boiled potatoes, staples everywhere on the island.

The star ratings in the restaurant listings below have been used to indicate the approximate cost per person in euros of a two-course meal with alcohol and a coffee:

★ Under €12
★★ €12–20
★★★ €20–35
★★★★ Over €35

FUNCHAL
Central Funchal
Mona Pizza ★
A great place to grab a pizza for lunch.
Rua das Pretas 45.
Tel: (291) 220372.

Arsénio's ★★
Pizza and fish restaurant, popular for its live *fado* singing and music.
Rua de Santa Maria 169.
Tel: (291) 224007.

Café do Museu ★★
Minimalist black tables and chairs under the

dark basalt arches of the Religious Art Museum and a menu of trendy international fish, meat and vegetarian dishes make this a fashionable setting for an evening meal or drinks.
Praça do Município.
Tel: (291) 281121.

Café do Teatro ★★
Occupying the last two arches of the Baltazar Dias Municipal Theatre, this trendy lunch- and nightspot serves soups, salads, coffee, wines and spirits out on the cobbles and indoors.
Avenida Arriaga.
Tel: (291) 226371.

Grand Café Golden Gate ★★
A Funchal institution with green shutters, wicker chairs and a colonial feel. One of the most atmospheric places to eat in town at any time of day.
Avenida Arriaga 29.
Tel: (291) 234383.

Le Jardin ★★
Old Town restaurant with French influences, specialising in flambéed fish and peppered steak.
Rua Dom Carlos I 60.
Tel: (291) 222864.

An eye-catching sign

Londres ★★
Despite the name, authentic Madeiran and mainland Portuguese cuisine is served here, with a different speciality each day of the week – a good place to sample *bacalhau* (salt cod), for which it is said there are as many recipes as there are days in the year.
Rua da Carreira 64A.
Tel: (291) 353329.

Marina Terrace ★★
Pizza, seafood and live entertainment with sea views. One of several good restaurants fronting the yacht marina, serving everything from pizza to lobster. Staff wear Madeiran costume and there is live music and

folk dancing nightly from around 7.30pm. *Marina do Funchal. Tel: (291) 230547.*

Marisa ★★

Another family-owned restaurant known for its Portuguese specialities, this one's are paella, *arroz de marisco,* spicy prawns and grilled beef. A small wooden balcony upstairs allows for al fresco dining. It is very small, so call ahead.

Rua de Santa Maria 22. Tel: (291) 226189.

O Portão ★★

Famous for its fish, meat and *bacalhau* (salt cod) dishes, the restaurant's tables spill out on to the terrace near the church, making this a great place to people-watch. Service is so friendly that by the end of the evening everyone will know your name.
Rua do Portão de São Tiago. Tel: (291) 221125.

Vagrant ★★

Also known as 'The Beatles' Boat' because it was once owned by the Fab Four, this now forms the centrepiece of Funchal's so-called 'Floating Restaurant' area; but do not worry if you suffer from seasickness – these boats are firmly bedded in concrete and their floating days are well and truly over. Despite the gimmicky ambience, you

Relaxing at pavement cafés in Funchal

can dine well here on pizza or typical Madeiran food at reasonable prices.
Avenida do Mar.
Tel: (291) 223572.

O Regional ★★/★★★
Best of a bunch of places near the Madeira Story Centre, serving very traditionally prepared Madeiran staples and fresh fish dishes in a light and spacious dining area.
Rua Dom Carlos I 54.
Tel: (291) 232956.

O Almirante ★★★
A very romantic, candlelit interior makes up for the traffic-laden front terrace. The dining room has an old-world feel with exposed wooden beams, chandeliers and high-backed chairs. Food and service are traditional and exquisite; dine on dishes such as *fígado à Madeira* (Madeira liver), lobster, squid and shark.
Largo do Poço 1–2.
Tel: (291) 224299.

Caravelha ★★★
Smart flambé restaurant with harbour views, and one of the few in Madeira to offer a specific vegetarian menu. *Arroz de marisco* (seafood risotto) is also a popular choice.
Avenida do Mar 15.
Tel: (291) 223695.

O Celeiro ★★★
Smart cellar-restaurant, ideal for a romantic candlelit dinner, serving fresh grilled fish, traditional Madeiran dishes and Brazilian-style cod.
Rua dos Aranhas 22.
Tel: (291) 230622.

Jango ★★★
A tiny Old Town restaurant which only seats 20 customers. It specialises in *arroz de marisco* (seafood risotto) and *cataplana*, a hearty fish stew.
Rua de Santa Maria 166.
Tel: (291) 221280.
Reservations essential.

Restaurante São Pedro ★★★
This contemporary eatery opposite the beautiful Church of St Peter has a menu heavy with Madeiran specialities and interesting décor. A handy lunch or dinner spot when visiting the Convent of St Clare.
Rua de São Pedro 2–4.
Tel: (291) 222217.

Molhe ★★★★
The restaurant takes its name from the rock outcrop upon which it is built. The vast amount of glass used in the design of this ultra-modern restaurant allows the best views across Funchal from the Forte de Nossa Senhora da Conceição. The food prepared by the award-winning chef is international with a Madeiran twist.
Forte de Nossa Senhora da Conceição.
Tel: 915 193034.
Reservations essential.

Hotel Zone
Beerhouse ★
Pub-style snack restaurant and bar.
São Lazaro.
Tel: (291) 229011.

The Prince Albert Pub ★
A lively Welsh-owned British pub with Sky Sports, pub grub, British beers and live music on Thursdays.
Rua da Imperatriz Dona Amélia. Tel: (291) 235793.

Doca do Cavacas ★★
Atmospheric restaurant specialising in seafood and fresh fish.

Ponta da Cruz, Estrada Monumental.
Tel: (291) 762057.

Moby Dick ★★

Situated near the ocean and the main road in an ugly courtyard between Reid's and the Lido, this not very pretty café is surprisingly good. The interior makes up for what the exterior lacks, and the food is excellent; seafood such as *gambas piri piri* (spiced prawns), vegetarian choices and what many consider to be the freshest fish in Funchal. An added plus, if you are not staying nearby the owner will pick you up (minimum four people).
Estrada Monumental 87.
Tel: (291) 776868.

Sol e Mar ★★

A lively and informal, good-value restaurant offering pizza, pasta and Madeiran dishes, including the must-try fish stew.
Flor do Lido Building, Estrada Monumental 314B. Tel: (291) 762227.

Summertime ★★

Great value for families with its location near the Lido Complex, making

it a rest break from swimming, with lunches and dinners of good-quality Portuguese dishes. Grown-ups will enjoy the terrace overlooking the ocean.
Estrada Monumental 21.
Tel: (291) 762476.

Villa Cliff ★★

Adjoining Reid's Hotel, this restaurant is recommended for its imaginative pasta dishes.
Estrada Monumental 169.
Tel: (291) 763025.

Casa dos Reis ★★★

Intimate restaurant behind the Savoy Hotel, serving French and international cuisine.
Rua da Penha de França 6. Tel: (291) 225182.

Armada ★★★★

This restaurant at the Royal Savoy is popular with Madeirans as well as visitors. Best described as East–West fusion cuisine, the food reflects the interior of the hotel, which has antiques everywhere collected from Portugal's exploration of Africa, the Far East and west towards South America.
Rua Carvalho Araújo.
Tel: (291) 213000.

Reservations recommended.

Casa Velha ★★★★

Elegant dining in a well-restored 19th-century town house; specialises in flambé dishes and lobster with pasta.
Rua da Imperatriz Dona Amélia 69.
Tel: (291) 205600.

Dona Amélia ★★★★

Elegant but pricey international-standard cuisine, set in a restored 19th-century town house with intimate terrace.
Rua da Imperatriz Dona Amélia 83.
Tel: (291) 225784.

Escola Profissional de Hotelaria ★★★★

Dine where Madeira's future chefs and waiters receive their exemplary training. The hotel school serves lunch, high tea and dinner. All expertly prepared and elegantly served by advanced-level students.
Travessa dos Piornais.
Tel: (291) 700386.
Dress: smart casual.
Reservations essential.

Les Faunes ★★★★

Probably Madeira's best restaurant, the haunt of visiting dignitaries and those who can afford a very special night out. The bright and airy dining room is simply decorated with drawings of fauns by Picasso. Formal evening dress is not compulsory but is worn by most of the guests.

Reid's Hotel, Estrada Monumental.
Tel: (291) 717100.
Reservations advised.

Il Gallo d'Oro ★★★★

The restaurant at the Cliff Bay Hotel was awarded Madeira's first and only Michelin star in 2009. The food is a gentle fusion of Mediterranean and Madeiran cuisine.

Estrada Monumental 147.
Tel: (291) 707700.
Evening dress required.
Reservations essential.

Reid's Dining Room ★★★★

Slightly less expensive than Les Faunes, but equally smart (evening dress advised), Reid's main dining room offers chandeliered elegance and a choice of reasonably priced set menus or more highly priced à la carte.

Reid's Hotel, Estrada Monumental.
Tel: (291) 763001.
Dinner only. Reservations essential.

Funchal environs

Hortensia Tea House ★★

On the Levada dos Tornos path, this delightful restaurant set in lush landscaped gardens with views across Funchal from its shaded terraces can also be reached from the road. It serves soup, cakes

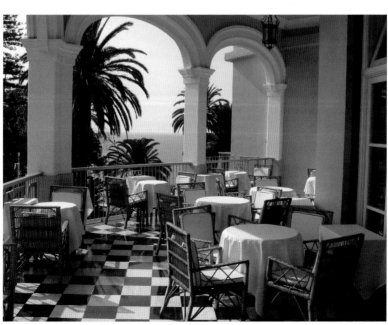

The tea terrace at Reid's Hotel

and light snacks for lunch, along with its famous apple pie.
Caminho dos Pretos 89. Tel: (291) 792179.

AROUND FUNCHAL
Câmara de Lobos
Vila do Peixe ★★★
The large, new, glass-fronted 'House of Fish' enjoys panoramic views of the harbour and Atlantic and is the best place in town for local and imported fish dishes.
Rua Dr João Abel de Freitas 30A. Tel: (291) 099909.

Monte
Café do Parque ★
Tucked away in a corner of Monte's main square, surrounded by tropical vegetation and shaded by tall trees, this is the best place to grab a quick snack.
Largo da Fonte. Tel: (291) 782880.

EASTERN MADEIRA
Caniço
A Lareira ★★
Located conveniently on the square in front of the church, here you can enjoy a mix of Madeiran

and international dishes in a rural-style dining room with real fire, or just a coffee and cake in the café opposite.
Estrada da Ponta Oliveira 2. Tel: (291) 934494.

La Terraça ★★
If it's honestly prepared Madeiran fare you hunger for, look no further than this restaurant near the church in Caniço. As the name suggests, the dining space is located on a covered terrace with superb views.
Rua João Paulo II 30. Tel: (291) 933898.

Machico
Baía ★
This contemporary café and restaurant has some fine outdoor seating overlooking the bobbing boats tied up in the marina and views back across the bay.
Porto de Recreio. Tel: (291) 966502.

O Galã ★★
The inexpensive O Galã is popular with locals and has a simple traditional interior, great al fresco dining in the narrow street outside and

a no-nonsense menu.
Rua General António Teixeira de Aguiar 1–7. Tel: (291) 965720.

Mercado Velho ★★
Housed in the old municipal market, this place with bags of character serves up meat and fish in equal measure, best consumed in the shady cobbled yard where tables and chairs cluster round an old fountain.
Mercado Velho de Machico. Tel: (291) 965926.

CENTRAL HIGHLANDS
Curral das Freiras
Eira do Serrado ★★★
This place is worth eating at for the terrific views, as it sits 500m (1,640ft) above Curral das Freiras, but it is also a great place for grilled meats and fish.
Eira do Serrado. Tel: (291) 710060.

Poiso
Casa de Abrigo ★★
On the crossroads at Poiso Pass this mountain restaurant is popular with hikers. The big open fire is welcoming here, as

Food and drink

the weather in the mountains can often be colder and wetter than elsewhere on the island, but it has another function too – *espetada* is prepared while you watch over the embers of the fire.
Poiso Pass.
Tel: (291) 782269.

Santana
O Pescador ★★★
The latest addition to Santana's culinary scene is this chic fish restaurant boasting contemporary design and an adventurous menu.
Pico António Fernandes.
Tel: (291) 572272.
Quinta do Furão ★★★
There are extensive views of the north coast from the restaurant terrace. Inside, the restaurant and pub are warmed by

open-hearth fires. Serves traditional Madeiran and Portuguese cuisine.
Achada do Gramacho.
Tel: (291) 570100.

WESTERN MADEIRA
Porto Moniz
Cachalote ★★
Possibly Madeira's most bizarre restaurant, the Cachalote perches on a platform of volcanic rock amid the town's famous sea pools. Enjoy fish and meat dishes in the huge downstairs dining room.
Ilhéumar.
Tel: (291) 853180.

Ribeira Brava
Dom Luís ★★
This outdoor restaurant serves a selection of traditional Madeiran fare plus pizzas and pastas. The service and views are

the most enviable in town.
Rua Marginal da Vila.
Tel: (291) 952543.
Borda D'Água ★★★
This slightly upmarket restaurant serves a wide choice of seafood dishes in clean-cut contemporary surroundings.
Rua Engenheiro Pereira Ribeiro. Tel: (291) 957697.

PORTO SANTO
Pé na Água ★★
This hip place set in the dunes just outside Vila Baleira is one of the coolest places to come in the evening to fill up on superb seafood.
Sítio das Pedras Pretas.
Tel: (291) 983114.
Teodorico ★★
A family-run restaurant where the locals go for the best *espetada* on the island.
Serra do Dentro.
Tel: (291) 982257.
Quinta do Serrado ★★★
A rustic-style restaurant built with traditional stone walls and a cosy open-hearth fire. Grilled octopus and stewed goat are the specialities.
Sítio do Pedregal.
Tel: (291) 980270.

Bright sunshades add to the ambience at a pavement café, Ribeira Brava

Accommodation

Madeira offers a wide choice in quality accommodation, ranging from venerable old hotels such as Reid's (see pp174–5) to inexpensive self-catering apartments. Package holiday prices are hard to beat, but you must book well in advance if you want to visit during the time school holidays are on, remembering that Madeira is as popular in winter as in summer: in fact, Christmas and New Year are the most expensive times to visit because of the festivities (see pp20–23).

If you book a package holiday, be sure to compare operators' prices because they vary quite a lot, even for identical rooms in the same hotel. Be careful, too, to check how far out of town the hotel is – some are up to 5km (3 miles) from the city centre, and though they offer a shuttle bus service, you will still feel isolated. Bear in mind that rates vary markedly according to the season.

Five-star hotels

All five-star establishments in Funchal occupy prime positions in the Hotel Zone and are less than ten minutes' walk from the city centre. They have splendid sea views, huge swimming pools and direct access to the sea with roped-off bathing areas. You will be charged €115–150 per night, plus a supplement for a room with a sea view, but you may consider this worthwhile, since rooms without sea views look on to the busy Estrada Monumental.

Three- and four-star hotels

Most of the island's hotels fall into this category and are located in the sprawl of high-rise developments stretching westwards from the city centre along the Estrada Monumental.

Nearly all the hotels have a pool, but these are rarely big enough for serious swimming, though the excellent Lido pool complex (*see* Sport and leisure, *p156*) is nearby. Nearly all the hotels are modern, and for approximately €55–80 per night you can usually count on your own balcony and bathroom, satellite TV, direct-dial telephones, plus a café, bar and small shop. Breakfast is nearly always included in the room price.

Quinta-style hotels

Many elegant *quintas* (or mansions) were demolished to make way for the high-rises of the Hotel Zone, but others thankfully survive and a few have been converted into elegant, antique-filled hotels set in well-tended gardens.

Self-catering

Funchal has many inexpensive apartments and apart-hotels for rent where the accommodation includes a small kitchen and a living/eating area – excellent if you want to take children or prepare your own meals. Private apartments with maid service are also available; look for classified advertisements in the travel sections of the weekend newspapers.

Budget accommodation

No-frills accommodation for about €25–50 per night is possible in a *pensão* (pension). These are often located above shops, bars or restaurants. The setting is not always tranquil, but the prices are ideal for anyone on a tight budget.

Beyond Funchal

Several towns along Madeira's southern coast have resort complexes which some visitors use as an alternative base for exploring the island, especially those who want to escape from the city and enjoy relative solitude. The island also has two *pousadas*, state-owned hotels, deliberately sited in isolated positions and popular with walkers. The 18-room **Pousada do Pico do Arieiro** (*tel: (291) 230110*) is located at the summit of Madeira's third-highest peak and is perfect for those who want to experience the silence of the mountains, the beauty of the night sky and the glowing light of the rising sun. The other is the **Pousada do Pico Ruivo** just below the peak of the island's

highest mountain. Both need booking several days in advance, or longer if you want to stay at the weekend.

The star ratings below indicate the price per double or twin room:

★	Under €60
★★	€60–100
★★★	€100–150
★★★★	Over €150

FUNCHAL

Buganvília Hotel ★

This hotel is located right in the centre of the Lido Complex and is very popular with families.
Rua da Casa Branca.
Tel: (291) 706615.

Four Views Monumental Lido ★★

Centrally located, this hotel is handy for the Lido Complex. There are views across

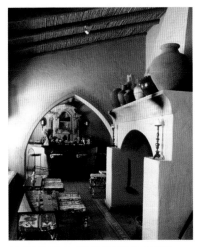

An old mansion converted into an elegant small hotel

the sea and the waterfront from the rooms on the upper levels and the pool terrace.

Estrada Monumental 284.
Tel: (291) 724000.

Hotel Savoy Gardens ★★
Set in a mature garden of frangipani, magnolia and flame trees and a riot of exotic flowers, this hotel has a fresh modern feel to it. Away from the busy Estrada Monumental it is quiet and secluded.

Azinhaga da Casa Branca.
Tel: (291) 213600.

Quinta Bela São Tiago ★★
At one time this *quinta* was the official residence of the vice-governor of Madeira. It was extended in keeping with the architectural heritage of the original building. Set in extensive gardens with a banana plantation and an orchard in the east of Funchal, it has an air of peacefulness.

Rua Bela de São Tiago.
Tel: (291) 204500.

Quinta das Vistas ★★★
Luxury and elegance ooze from this *quinta*. Surrounded by extensive terraced gardens and a nine-hole golf course, it occupies an enviable position on top of a small hill with extensive views over Funchal from the pool terrace and the south-facing rooms.

Caminho de Santo António 52A.
Tel: (291) 750007.

Reid's Palace ★★★★
Set in subtropical gardens on a clifftop overlooking the Atlantic Ocean and Funchal, this legendary hotel is the last word in luxury and service, and still has a colonial air about it (*see also pp174–5*).

Estrada Monumental 139.
Tel: (291) 717171.

Royal Savoy ★★★★
A modern hotel with an excellent seafront pool area and direct access to the sea. The interior is packed with antiques, some of them almost museum pieces, from the days of Portuguese exploration and trade around the world.

Rua Carvalho Araújo.
Tel: (291) 213000.

AROUND FUNCHAL
Câmara de Lobos
Quinta do Estreito ★★★
Reflecting the colonial style of architecture, this *quinta* is set in the hills. Decorated in a classical style throughout, there is an air of peacefulness, enhanced by the unobtrusive friendliness of the staff.

Rua José Joaquim da Costa.
Tel: (291) 910350.

EASTERN MADEIRA
Camacha
Quinta do Serrado ★★★
There is an appealing rustic charm about this modern *quinta*. Built in the local basaltic stone and with generous use of timber, it is set in natural surroundings away from the developments along the beach, which gives it an atmosphere of exclusivity and tranquillity.

Camacha.
Tel: (291) 980270.

Machico
Dom Pedro Baía ★
On the waterfront of Machico, with the mountains sweeping up from behind it, this hotel is popular with those wanting to escape the bustle and tourist traps of Funchal. Madeira

Oceanos, a diving centre where you can hire equipment, go on a dive or learn to dive with a certified instructor, is based at this hotel.
Estrada de São Roque.
Tel: (291) 969500.

Santo da Serra
Enotel Golf Hotel ★
A modern hotel in a restored traditional Madeiran manor house next to the Santo da Serra golf course. The tranquil setting in grounds that include forest, gardens and parkland makes it ideal for those seeking a quiet and relaxing holiday.
Sítio dos Casais Próximos.
Tel: (291) 550550.

CENTRAL HIGHLANDS
Curral das Freiras
Estalgem Eira do Serrado ★
A modern hotel with probably the most impressive, and certainly the most precipitous, views in Madeira, as it looks down on the village of Curral das Freiras. The restaurant has stunning views but

you certainly need a head for heights.
Curral das Freiras.
Tel: (291) 710060.

WESTERN MADEIRA
Ponta do Sol
Enotel Baia ★★★
Located in a quiet seafront location, this hotel has been designed around a row of converted, typical Madeiran town houses. The interior design is chic and modern.
Rua Dr João Augusto Teixeira.
Tel: (291) 970149.

Porto Moniz
Pensão Salgueiro ★
Located on a seafront roundabout, this *pensão* (pension) is across the road from Porto Moniz's natural rock pools.
Lugar do Tenente 34.
Tel: (291) 850080.

Ribeira Brava
Vinháticos Pousada ★
On the old road to Boca da Encumeada, this guest house is surrounded by mountains and laurisilva forest. There are some great views down the steep, terraced valley to

Ribeira Brava and the sea.
Serra de Água.
Tel: (291) 952344.

PORTO SANTO
Pestana Porto Santo ★★★
The newest hotel on the island, it consists of a series of 'villas' surrounding gardens and two free-form swimming pools, one with fresh water and one with sea water. There are a few private villas, each with its own private plunge pool. The hotel also has direct access to the beach.
Sitio do Campo de Baixo.
Tel: (291) 144000.

Hotel Porto Santo ★★★★
The first hotel built on the island and the one with the latest facilities in the form of the GeoMedicine Centre (*see pp136–7*), a luxury spa that makes use of the unique properties of Porto Santo's sand. New private suites that feel more like villas are designed for maximum privacy. Well-kept gardens lead down to the beach and an excellent beach bar.
Campo de Baixo.
Tel: (291) 980140.

Reid's Hotel

Reid's is one of those legendary hotels which nearly everyone has heard of, the sort of place which regularly entertains Hollywood film stars, royalty and heads of state. The hotel buildings resemble a cross between a colonial gentlemen's club and an aristocrat's home.

In rags-to-riches fashion, the hotel was founded by William Reid, one of twelve children of an impoverished Scottish crofter. Reid set off in 1836 to make his fortune, and worked his passage on board ship to Madeira, where he met William Wilkinson. They set up an agency catering to the needs of Madeira's wealthy foreign visitors, most of whom would hire a *quinta* (a large house and garden) for the duration of their stay, relying on Reid to find a suitable property and furnish it according to their tastes. The money Reid made enabled him to buy *quintas* and convert them into residential hotels; eventually he bought the plot of land on which Reid's Hotel now sits, enjoying a prime clifftop position with wonderful sea views.

William Reid did not live to see his dream fulfilled – he died in 1888, aged 66, while the hotel was under construction – but his sons took over and opened the doors of this luxury hotel to the first paying guests in 1891.

British Prime Minister Winston Churchill was just one of the many regular guests who would arrive by sea at the hotel's private landing stage, to be carried by lift to the upper gardens, immaculately tended and filled with palms. Other famous guests include Captain Scott, who stayed here on his way to Antarctica, George Bernard Shaw, who learnt to tango here and Empress Elisabeth of Austria, who came to mourn the suicide of her son Prince Rudolf. Arrival at the hotel was either from the liners that stopped off at Funchal or by the flying boat service from Southampton. To this very day, the hotel is best seen from the sea.

Even if you cannot afford to stay at Reid's, you can still enjoy the hushed ambience and impeccable service by splashing out on afternoon tea (Madeira cake and cucumber sandwiches with the crusts removed). The poolside buffet lunch is another way of taking in the hotel's style, or you can sip Madeira in the cocktail bar. Just remember to dress smartly, though, or you might be politely turned away – the hotel no longer insists that evening dress be worn for dinner, but it does suggest that you might feel conspicuous if you do not.

Reid's Hotel is perched on the clifftops overlooking the Bay of Funchal and the Atlantic

Practical guide

Arriving

By air

The cheapest way to get to Madeira is by chartered flight. Tour operators and handling agents (Triam, Servisair and TAP) specialising in Madeira offer direct flights to Funchal as part of a hotel and flight package, but many of them also offer inexpensive flight-only deals.

TAP (Air Portugal), the national carrier, also offers scheduled flights direct to Funchal as well as via Lisbon (*www.flytap.com*), and **easyJet** now flies from Bristol and Stansted to Funchal (*www.easyjet.com*).

Airport facilities

Funchal's airport is small and efficient, and lies 18km (1¼ miles) outside the city. You will rarely experience delays except in very severe weather. There is a viewing platform on the roof of the terminal building and all the usual airport facilities: a small duty-free shop, a currency exchange bureau, several car hire agencies plus bars and cafés.

City link

Transport from the airport to your hotel is usually included in package tours. If not, there are taxis available just outside the terminal exit doors to get to central Funchal. There is a very cheap bus that calls at the airport at regular intervals throughout the day. The drive to Funchal takes 20–30 minutes by taxi, 60 minutes by bus.

By sea

British, Russian and Norwegian cruise liners regularly visit the island as part of a week-long tour of the Canary Islands, Madeira and North Africa. Cruise passengers rarely get more than 24 hours on Madeira, scarcely long enough to sample the island's varied attractions, but some cruise companies allow you to take just part of the cruise, perhaps arriving in Madeira romantically by sea and returning home by air.

There are ferry services in the summer from Portimão in Portugal to Funchal operated by **Naviera Armas** (*www.navieraarmas.com*).

Entry formalities

The rules for entering Madeira are the same as those for the Portuguese mainland: citizens of other European Union (EU) member states don't require a visa; those from the USA, Canada, Australia and New Zealand can stay for up to 90 days without a visa. You will need to show your passport on entry; you will also need it when registering at hotels or changing money and traveller's cheques.

Travellers who require visas should obtain them in their country of residence.

Camping

Officially, camping in the mountains and forests is illegal on Madeira. There are two designated campsites on the island: **Parque de Campismo Porto Moniz** (*tel: (291) 850193 or (291) 853447*) and **Parque de Campismo Porto Santo** (*tel: (291) 982160 or (291) 982361*). Both are inexpensive and very basic; a piece of grass to pitch your tent, loos and cold showers only. These campsites have limited space, so it's best to book well in advance if planning to visit in July and August.

Children

For advice on enjoying Madeira with children, *see pp154–5*.

Climate

Funchal has an almost perfect climate; temperatures do not vary much from an average of 22°C (72°F) throughout the year, making it a perfect place to escape from the cold of northern European winters or the excessive heat of summer. Funchal and other towns on the south side of the island receive very little rain, except in autumn. The weather on the rest of the island is variable, depending on altitude and aspect with the north receiving most of the rain, and rain-clouds hanging almost permanently at the 800–1,000m (2,600–3,300ft) level (*see pp8–9 for further information*).

Conversion tables

See p179.

Clothes and shoe sizes in Madeira follow the standard sizes used in the rest of Europe.

FUNCHAL

October–March

April–September

WEATHER CONVERSION CHART

25.4mm = 1 inch

°F = 1.8 × °C + 32

Crime

Crime is an evil that has yet to take root in Madeira. Within the island's close-knit communities still strongly influenced by the teachings of the Roman Catholic Church, serious crimes are so rare as to be profoundly shocking when they do occur. Even so, you should not offer an invitation to crime by being careless with your valuables; use your hotel safe and do not leave possessions in unattended cars.

Do report crime at once if you fall victim to it – the police will do everything possible to help (*see Police p185*).

Customs

As Madeira is part of the EU, visitors from its member countries benefit from regulations introduced in 1993 that abolished the limits on duty-paid goods you could bring home as long as they were for personal use. This is only restricted by notional limits, above which you may be asked to prove that your purchases are for personal rather than commercial use.

EU Citizens aged 17 or over can bring back: 3,200 cigarettes, 400 cigarillos, 200 cigars, 3kg (6½lb) of tobacco, 110 litres of wine, 10 litres of spirits, 20 litres of fortified wine (or 26 bottles of Madeira) and 110 litres of beer.

Visitors to Madeira coming from non-EU countries are still eligible for duty-free allowances. The allowances are (per person aged over 17): 200 cigarettes or 100 cigarillos or 50 cigars or 250g (9oz) of tobacco; 1 litre of spirits and 2 litres of fortified or sparkling wine; 4 litres of table wine; 60cl (20fl oz) of perfume.

These limits may vary from time to time, so it is best to check when you make your purchase; current limits are posted in duty-free shops.

Driving

Renting a car gives you the flexibility to explore the island at your own pace. Bear in mind, though, that the daily cost of car hire is about the same as hiring a taxi for the day, with the advantage that the taxi driver takes the strain of the island's steep and tortuous roads. Remember that if you do hire a car, the driver will see little of the countryside. Total concentration is needed to avoid the myriad hazards, which include hairpin bends without crash barriers, roads so narrow that only one car can pass, and sheep in the middle of the road.

An expressway which now extends from the airport, around Funchal, and as far as Ribeira Brava, makes driving a bit easier. Most drivers are courteous, and they rarely break the speed limits of 60kph (37mph) in built-up areas and 90kph (56mph) elsewhere. Cars drive on the right, seat belts must be worn, and children under 12 are not allowed in the front seats. The more expensive hotels provide covered parking. Public car parks are located beneath the Marina Shopping Centre on Avenida do Mar and on the site of the old bus station near the Zona Velha. You pay by the hour, but the cost is reasonable. Outside Funchal free parking places are easy to find.

There are plenty of petrol stations in Funchal, including one that is open virtually around the clock on Avenida do Infante, nearly opposite the Carlton Park Hotel. It is a good idea to fill your tank before driving to the interior or north of the island where petrol stations are few and far between.

Warning triangles must be used if you break down, positioned in the road to the rear of the car. There are orange SOS call points at regular intervals beside main roads – walk to the nearest, press the button and wait for the rescue service to answer. Alternatively, car rental companies

Practical guide

will give you a telephone number that you can use to call out their own rescue service.

Car rental

If you do decide to explore Madeira at your own pace by car, be sure to book well in advance for the peak summer period (July, August and September), and for Christmas and New Year.

Look out too for the special 'Flydrive' packages organised by travel agencies, which allow you to tour the island, staying in a different hotel every night, and include the cost of car rental.

To hire a car you must be over 21 years of age, with one or two years' driving experience, a driving licence from your own country or an international driving licence, as well as a passport. You must keep your passport with you at all times while driving. Seat belts are to be worn at all times. Madeira has very strict laws on drinking and driving. Each car hire agency has its own policies regarding payment, but most will not accept cash and require a credit card.

Auto Jardim Funchal Airport.
Tel: (291) 524023.
www.auto-jardim.com
Avis Funchal Airport.
Tel: (291) 524392.
www.avis.com
Largo Antonio Nobre 164, Funchal.
Tel: (291) 764546.
Hotel Monumental Lido, Funchal.
Tel: (291) 764546.

CONVERSION TABLE

FROM	TO	MULTIPLY BY
Inches	Centimetres	2.54
Feet	Metres	0.3048
Yards	Metres	0.9144
Miles	Kilometres	1.6090
Acres	Hectares	0.4047
Gallons	Litres	4.5460
Ounces	Grams	28.35
Pounds	Grams	453.6
Pounds	Kilograms	0.4536
Tons	Tonnes	1.0160

To convert back, for example from centimetres to inches, divide by the number in the third column.

MEN'S SUITS

UK	36	38	40	42	44	46	48
Rest of Europe	46	48	50	52	54	56	58
USA	36	38	40	42	44	46	48

DRESS SIZES

UK	8	10	12	14	16	18
France	36	38	40	42	44	46
Italy	38	40	42	44	46	48
Rest of Europe	34	36	38	40	42	44
USA	6	8	10	12	14	16

MEN'S SHIRTS

UK	14	14.5	15	15.5	16	16.5	17
Rest of Europe	36	37	38	39/40	41	42	43
USA	14	14.5	15	15.5	16	16.5	17

MEN'S SHOES

UK	7	7.5	8.5	9.5	10.5	11
Rest of Europe	41	42	43	44	45	46
USA	8	8.5	9.5	10.5	11.5	12

WOMEN'S SHOES

UK	4.5	5	5.5	6	6.5	7
Rest of Europe	38	38	39	39	40	41
USA		6	6.5	7	7.5	8	8.5

Budget Funchal Airport.
Tel: (291) 524661. www.budget.com
Hotel Duas Torres, Estrada
Monumental 239, Funchal.
Tel: (291) 766518. Fax: (291) 765619.
Hertz Funchal Airport.
Tel: (291) 523040. Fax: (291) 523017.
www.hertz.com
Centro Comercial Lido Loja 1, Estrada
Monumental, Funchal.
Tel: (291) 764410. Fax: (291) 764452.
Sixt Rent-A-Car Funchal Airport.
Tel: (291) 523355. www.sixt.pt

Electricity

The standard supply on Madeira is 220
volts. Your appliance will work if it is
fitted with a two-pin plug; otherwise an
adaptor is needed.

Embassies and consulates

UK Rua da Alfândega 10, Funchal.
Tel: (291) 212860.
USA Rua da Alfândega 10, Funchal.
Tel: (291) 235636.

Emergency numbers

Universal: *Tel: 112.*
Hospital(s): *Tel: (291) 705600 or
(291) 705730.*

Health

Take care in the sun, whether out
walking or by the pool. You can get
burnt very quickly, as the sun is more
intense than you might think, despite
the relatively low temperatures.

If you do have a health problem, you
can safely put yourself in the hands of

the island's well-trained English-
speaking doctors. **Dr Zino** (*Avenida do
Infante 26. Tel: (291) 742227*) has a
practice close to the Hotel Zone and is
used by all tour operators.

If you seek medical treatment,
remember to keep all bills and receipts in
order to claim on your travel insurance
policy. All EU countries have reciprocal
arrangements for reclaiming the cost of
medical services. UK residents should
obtain the European Health Insurance
Card from any UK post office. The card
and your passport must be presented
before treatment is sought at the
Serviço de Migrantes (*Centro de Saúde
do Bom Jesus, Rua das Hortas 67. Tel:
(291) 229161. Open: Mon–Fri
9.30am–noon & 2–4pm*).

Outside Funchal, nearly every
community has a health centre (*Centro
de Saúde*), where help can be sought,
and there are emergency services
(*urgências*) at the health centres in
Ribeira Brava, Calheta, São Vicente,
Porto Moniz, Santana and Machico. On
Porto Santo, the centre is at Vila Baleira.

Madeira has no mandatory
vaccination requirements, and no
vaccination recommendations other
than to keep tetanus and polio
immunisation up to date. Like every
other part of the world, AIDS is present.

The food and water on the island are
safe to consume.

Lost property

There is a good chance that any
property you lose (especially if left in a

taxi or bus) will be handed in to the lost property office in Funchal: contact **Polícia de Perdas & Achados** (*Rua da Infância 28. Tel: (291) 208200*).

Maps

Perfectly adequate maps of Funchal and Madeira are given out free by the tourist office at *Avenida Arriaga 18, Funchal*. For walking, *Landscapes of Madeira* (4th edition) by John and Pat Underwood is the indispensable guide, with routes plotted on to Portuguese contoured military maps.

For driving, the Bartholomew *Madeira Holiday Map* is the most up to date, showing roads that are under construction and due to open in the years ahead.

When reading Madeiran maps, it is useful to know the meaning of certain place-name elements:

achada plateau
arco curving mountain ridge
boca mouth/mountain pass
cabo cape
caldeirão crater or basin
calheta stream
caminho path and (confusingly) road
cruzinhas crossroads
encumeada summit
fonte spring
jardim garden
levada irrigation canal
lombada ridge
miradouro viewpoint
monte mount
parque park
praça square

ribeira river/river valley
rocha rock/crag
vale valley

Media

Madeira's main daily newspaper is the *Diário de Notícias*. This produces a four-page English-language supplement which is distributed to most hotels and which summarises local and world news. It also contains a miscellany of information on everything – the weather, exchange rates, the day's TV and radio schedules, which cruise liners are in harbour and what is on at the local cinemas and theatre.

Supplementing this is the monthly *Madeira Island Bulletin*, free from hotels and the tourist office, which contains lots of useful information on restaurants, shops and entertainment.

On the radio you can pick up the BBC World Service and listen to hourly news reports. Madeira Tourist Radio 96MHz FM (in English) broadcasts every day, except Sunday, at 5.45pm. The main theme of the show is restaurant recommendations; keep in mind that it is a commercial station where businesses pay for advertisements.

Most hotels in Funchal have satellite facilities, so you can usually pick up 20 or so channels, including the American CNN channel, for news.

A wide range of English newspapers and magazines can be bought in hotel shops or city centre newsagents, usually the day after publication.

Language

Most Madeirans speak basic English and the staff of shops, hotels and restaurants will be fluent. It is worth knowing some basic Portuguese phrases, however, since you are likely to hear them spoken a lot, and you may even want to try them out yourself. Remember that in Portuguese the letter s is pronounced like the s in sugar unless it is followed by a vowel; thus *carros* (car) is pronounced *carroosh*. The letter z sounds similar, so *se faz favor* (please) is pronounced *suh fash favor*. When the tilde accent (~) appears above the letters ao (as in *pão* – bread) it sounds like ow followed by a slight oo (*powoo*).

Useful words and phrases

hello	olá	**white**	branco
goodbye	adeus	**red**	tinto
good morning	bom dia	**rosé**	rosé
good afternoon	boa tarde	**green (young)**	verde
good evening	boa noite	**sparkling**	espumante
please	por favor/se faz favor	**bottle**	garrafa
thank you	obrigada (F)	**half bottle**	meia garrafa
	obrigado (M)	**tea**	chá
yes/no	sim/não	**lemon**	limão
do you speak English?	fala inglês?	**fizzy mineral water**	água com gás
how are you?	como está?	**still mineral water**	água sem gás
very well	muito bem	**orange juice**	sumo de laranja
how much?	quanto custa?	**coffee (espresso)**	bica
very good	muito bom	**coffee (large, strong and black)**	café grande
excuse me	com licença		
sorry/pardon me	desculpe	**coffee (large, weak and black)**	carioca
it does not matter	não faz mal		
good luck	boa sorte	**coffee with milk (large cup) (literally 'a Chinese lady')**	chinesa
In bars/cafés			
I would like (a beer)	queria (cerveja)		
please	se faz favor	**coffee with milk (small cup)**	garota
Cheers (your health)	saúde		
enjoy your meal	bom apetite	**coffee with much milk (tall glass) (literally 'a galleon')**	galão
the bill please	a conta, se faz favor		
wine	vinho		
house wine	vinho da casa	**sugar**	açúcar

Food

breakfast	pequeno almoço
lunch	almoço
high tea (meal)	lanche
dinner	jantar
bread	pão
cake	bolo
cheese	queijo
chicken	frango
eggs	ovos
fish	peixe
fruit	fruta
ham	fiambre
ice cream	gelado
lamb	borrego
pork	porco
rice	arroz
shellfish	mariscos
steak	bife
tuna	atum
veal	vitela

Out and about

airport	aeroporto
beach	praia
bus station	estação de autocarros
bus stop	paragem
cake shop	pastelaria
chemist	farmácia
church	igreja
danger	perigo/risco
doctor	médico
market	mercado
petrol station	posto de gasolina
police station	posto de polícia
post office	correios
supermarket	supermercado
swimming pool	piscina
telephone	telefone
tourist information	poste de turismo
toilet	quarto de banho
(men/women)	(senhores/senhoras)

A selection of vintage bottles of Madeira

Money matters

The money used on Madeira is the euro, which is divided into 100 cents. There are seven denominations of the euro note: €5, €10, €20, €50, €100, €200 and €500; eight denominations of coins: 1 cent, 2 cents, 5 cents, 10 cents, 20 cents, 50 cents and €1 and €2.

Banks and currency exchange

All banks in Funchal offer currency exchange services and their rates are better than those of exchange bureaux or hotels. Banks are open Monday to Friday 8.30am–3pm, Saturday 9am–1pm, and several of the larger banks, located near the Sé (Cathedral) in Avenida Arriaga, have hole-in-the-wall exchange machines which operate 24 hours a day.

Exchange bureaux are open Monday to Friday 9am–1pm and 2–7pm, and Saturday 9am–1pm. Whether you use a bank or a bureau, you have to present your passport when changing money, even for cash transactions. It pays to exchange as much as possible at one go, since there is a standard tax per transaction, no matter how large or small.

Cheques and credit cards

Traveller's cheques, Eurocheques and all the major credit cards can be used for obtaining money. Traveller's cheques and Eurocheques may also be used for paying bills in the more upmarket, tourist-oriented hotels, shops and

The Porto Santo ferry

restaurants, but credit cards are not yet accepted at all places.

For small-value transactions and in inexpensive local restaurants, cash is king. Surprisingly, even some hotels and restaurants with pretensions to status have yet to join the credit card age.

Value added tax

Value added tax is levied on most luxury goods at rates in excess of 4 per cent. So long as you come from a country outside the EU, you can claim a refund of this tax on large purchases in shops that participate in the Tax Free Shopping scheme; they will have all the necessary forms (*see* Global Refund, *www.globalrefund.com*).

National holidays

1 January New Year's Day
February Shrove Tuesday
March–April Good Friday
25 April Revolution Day
April/May Corpus Christi
1 May Labour Day
10 June Portugal Day

1 **July** Discovery of Madeira Day
15 **August** Assumption
21 **August** General Holiday
5 **October** Republic Day
1 **November** All Saints' Day,
   Independence
1 **December** Restoration Day
8 **December** Feast of the Immaculate
   Conception
25 **December** Christmas Day

Opening hours

Banks Monday to Friday 8.30am–3pm.
Church 8am–1pm and 4–7pm but
these can be subject to local variation.
Exchange bureaux (*Cambios*) Monday
to Friday 9am–1pm and 2–7pm,
Saturday 9am–1pm.
Shops Monday to Friday 9am–1pm
and 3–7pm, Saturday 9am–1pm. These
hours are observed strictly by most
shops in central Funchal, but the
supermarket chains such as Lido Sol
and Nova Esperança are open
10am–9pm/10pm, seven days a week.

Pharmacies

In Portuguese a chemist or pharmacy is
called a *farmácia*. They display a sign
consisting of a white cross on a green
background and are open Monday to
Friday 9am–1pm and 3–7pm, Saturday
9am–1pm. All pharmacies have a notice
showing which is on 24-hour duty.

The centrally situated **Botica Inglesa**
(*Rua Câmara Pesteria 23–25. Tel: (291)
203060*) caters to English-speaking
visitors. There is also a pharmacy on-
call service (*tel: 118*).

Places of worship

Most Madeirans are Roman Catholic
and Mass is held regularly in churches
all around the island. Madeira has its
own Anglican chaplain and services are
held at the Church of the Holy Trinity
(better known as the English Church –
see pp42–3) (*Rua do Quebra Costas 18.
Tel: (291) 220674*), at 11am every
Sunday; refreshments are served
afterwards in the well-tended church
gardens. The times of other services are
posted in hotels and at the Tourist
Information Office, Avenida Arriaga 18.

Baptist services are held in English
on Sundays at 11am at Alto da Peno
126, Rua Silvestre, Quintino Frectas.
Catholic Mass is said in English at the
Igreja da Penha, on Rua Carvalho
Araújo at 10.30am on Sundays.

Police

The fact that the police keep a low
profile on Madeira is a tribute to the
law-abiding nature of most Madeirans,
but the police are there when you need
them. Dial 112 in an emergency,
otherwise (291) 222022. You can
approach police officers for information
or assistance: those with a red armband
are there to help visitors; they speak
another language as well as Portuguese
– in most cases this means English.

Postal services

Funchal's main post office (*correios*) is
centrally located just up from the statue
of Zarco on Avenida Zarco. Most of the
staff here speak English. As well as

postal transactions, you can also make overseas telephone calls from here, using special booths which enable you to pay once your call is finished.

The post office is open Monday to Friday 9am–1pm and 3–7pm, Saturday 9am–1pm, while the telephone booths stay open until 10pm. In the hotel district, there is also a post office in the **Lido Sol** supermarket complex (*Estrada Monumental 318*), which is open Monday to Friday 9am–7pm.

Public transport
Taxis
Madeira's yellow cabs are an easy, cheap way of getting about Funchal. There are ranks at central points in the Hotel Zone and in the city centre, and you can hail any cab displaying a *livre* (free) sign. Hotels and restaurants will call a cab for you or you can phone for one yourself (*tel: (291) 222000* or *(291) 222500*). Journeys are metered within Funchal. There are set rates for longer journeys to specific destinations around the island. The official price list should be available for consultation in the taxi; copies are also displayed in the Tourist Information Office, *Avenida Arriaga 18*, and in many hotels.

In theory the rates are also fixed for hiring a cab for the day or half-day, but in practice you can usually bargain the price down substantially. Hiring a taxi by the day means that you can work out your own tour itinerary, and if three or four people travel together this is cheaper than renting a self-drive car or joining an organised coach tour. Ask your hotel. Otherwise, ring **Taxis Madeira** (*tel: (291) 764476*). Try to book taxi tours a day or two in advance: good drivers are in demand.

Most taxi drivers are honest (but *see p27*); if you feel you have been treated badly you should record the driver's number (displayed on the dashboard and painted on the outside of the front doors). Reporting him to the police is a serious matter – simply to threaten to report the driver is probably sufficient to ensure a change of attitude.

Do not, under any circumstances, use unlicensed cabs whose smooth-talking drivers are out to rip you off, either through extortionate fares or by acting as touts for timeshare developments or other attractions.

Buses
If you intend to use buses (*autocarros*), be sure you have a lot of time and do not mind close contact with the local people, since they can get crowded. Orange town buses offer a very cheap way of getting around Funchal. The Tourist Office (*see p189*) has a leaflet giving times and routes. The destination is indicated at the front of the bus. You can pay when you board, but it is cheaper to buy tickets in advance in bulk from bus company kiosks on Avenida do Mar – the best deal is a seven-day pass available to visitors only, so you must produce your passport when you buy the ticket.

Long-distance buses are a useful form of transport for anyone who wants to explore Madeira's *levada* footpaths, since the bus system reaches most parts of the island far more cheaply than taxis. The problem is that the system is very confusing to the ordinary visitor. You will find full details of routes and timetables in the daily English supplements to the *Diário de Notícias* newspaper (distributed free to many hotels), but you will need the following information to work out which bus goes from where:

Rodoeste buses (red, grey and white) (*Tel: (291) 220148*), operating routes 1, 4, 6, 7, 96, 107, 139, 148 and 154, leave from the Rua Ribeira João Gomes in Funchal.

SAM buses (cream and green) (*Tel: (291) 201150*), operating routes 20, 23, 53, 60, 78, 113 and 156, depart from Rua Calouste Gulbenkian and service the east and northeast of the island, including the airport.

Three companies operate routes 2, 29, 77, 103, 136 and 155. Ask your hotel concierge, or enquire at the Tourist

Country bus stop

Information Office, Avenida Arriaga 18, for the latest information on these bus routes and companies.

Senior citizens

Senior citizens' concessions in Madeira are available only to Portuguese nationals.

Student/youth travel

If you are visiting Madeira on a budget, go for lower-cost flights via Lisbon rather than the more expensive direct flights, travel by bus and shop for food in local markets. Cheap rooms can be had in *pensões* (pensions) in most villages, though Funchal is geared to the upmarket traveller.

Some visitors to Madeira prefer to camp (*see* Camping, *pp176–7*) at one of the two designated campsites. Bear in mind that although sleeping under the stars might be peaceful and beautiful, it is illegal on Madeira and you could face expensive fines.

Sustainable tourism

Thomas Cook is a strong advocate of ethical and fairly traded tourism and believes that the travel experience should be as good for the places visited as it is for the people who visit them. That's why we firmly support The Travel Foundation: a charity that develops solutions to help improve and protect holiday destinations, their environment, traditions and culture. To find out what you can do to make a positive difference to the places you travel to and the people who live there, please visit *www.thetravelfoundation.org.uk*

Telecommunications

Local calls are easily made from coin-operated phones which take 20- and 50-cent and euro coins. For international calls, it is cheapest to buy a card from post offices and shops displaying the Credifone symbol and use the card phones to be found all over Funchal.

Alternatively, you can use the metered telephone booths at the main post office (*see* Postal services, *p186*) and pay at the end of your call. You can, of course, dial direct from your hotel room, and pay a hefty premium for the convenience.

To call another country dial *00* followed by the country code, then the area code, minus the initial *0*, then the subscriber number.

Australia *0061*
Ireland *00353*
New Zealand *0064*
South Africa *0027*
USA and **Canada** *001*
UK *0044*
Directory Enquiries (Madeira) *118*
Operator *090*
International Operator *171*

Internet

Internet access is good and is available in most hotels and is often free to use. A few hotels provide free in-room connection. In Central Funchal there are public Wi-fi hotspots to supplement those found in cafés and hotels. For those places that do charge the average rate is €5 per hour.

Mobiles

Despite being a very mountainous island, Madeira's mobile network coverage is excellent, with most towns and villages able to receive a signal. It is not a good idea to rely on a mobile phone while walking in the more remote areas, however, as the signal can be weak or non-existent.

Time

Madeira observes Greenwich Mean Time (GMT) in winter (end of September to end of March) and GMT plus 1 hour in summer and is in the same time zone as the UK and the Republic of Ireland. Thus in summer Madeira is 5 hours ahead of Eastern Standard Time, 8 hours ahead of Pacific Time, 1 hour behind Lisbon and much of Europe, 2 hours behind South Africa, 9 behind Australia and 12 behind New Zealand.

Tipping

On Madeira, nobody demands tips as a right or treats you differently if you do not tip – indeed, people seem pleasantly surprised when a tip is offered to them. It is normal to tip 10–15 per cent in bars and restaurants. Many expensive restaurants also include a 10 per cent service charge

Toilets

Hotels, bars, restaurants and museums have toilets for public use, and these are usually modern and clean.

Tourist information

Funchal's Tourist Information Office is centrally located (*Avenida Arriaga 18. Tel: (291) 211900. Open: Mon–Fri 9am–8pm, Sat 9am–6pm*).

The English-speaking staff are genuinely helpful and will supply free maps as well as answers to just about any question you may have. Within the office there is also a currency exchange bureau and a booking desk for organised tours.

There are smaller offices in the arrivals lounge at the airport and also in Machico, at Nossa Senhora do Amparo Fort (*tel: (291) 962289*).

Tourist offices overseas

There are Portuguese National Tourist Offices in many cities around the world, including:

Canada 60 Bloor St West, Suite 1005, Toronto, Ontario M4W 3B8. *Tel: +1 416 921 7376.*
UK 11 Belgrave Square, London SW1X 8PP. *Tel: (020) 7201 6633.*
USA 590 Fifth Avenue, 4th Floor, New York, NY 10036-4704. *Tel: +1 (212) 723 0200.*

Travel agents

There are numerous travel agents in the Hotel Zone and in central Funchal and they will help you choose the coach excursions, boat trips, *levada* walking

tours or jeep safaris that are best for you. The following are among the leading agents and operators:
Blandy's Everything from island tours to folk evenings or mini cruises (*Avenida Zarco 2. Tel: (291) 200620*).
Madeira Explorers Levada & Leisure Walks Trained guides lead walking tours of Madeira's *levadas*, mountains and ridges (*Centro Comercial Monumental Lido, 3rd floor, Shop 5, Estrada Monumental. Tel: (291) 763701. www.madeira-levada-walks.com*).
Strawberry World This is one-stop shopping for Madeira: from car hire, bus tours, walks and mountain climbing to restaurants and accommodation. The company offers many types of holiday packages (*Centro Comercial Monumental Lido, 3rd floor, Office 2, Estrada Monumental. Tel: (291) 762421. www.strawberry-world.com*).
Terras de Adventura (Trails of Adventure) This company is definitely for the thrill seekers; choose from sea kayaking, diving, parasailing or mountain climbing, jeep safaris and four-wheel biking (*Caminho do Amparo 25. Tel: (291) 266818 or (291) 261018. www.madeira-island.com/aventura*).

Travellers with disabilities

Facilities for visitors with disabilities are limited. TAP (Air Portugal) has provision for passengers with wheelchairs, and luxury hotels such as the Savoy and Madeira Palácio are able to offer suitable accommodation, as can the Luamar Hotel on Porto Santo.

Index

Acknowledgements

Thomas Cook Publishing wishes to thank the photographers, picture libraries and other organisations, to whom the copyright belongs, for the photographs in this book.

AA PHOTO LIBRARY/PETER BAKER 9, 30, 35, 83, 125, 157, 159; JON WYAND 8, 15, 21, 34, 36, 37, 39, 44, 45, 51, 52, 53, 58, 59, 60, 62, 63, 68, 69, 71a, 74, 75, 78, 79, 82a, 82b, 84, 86, 87, 88, 93, 99, 104, 108, 109, 113, 114, 115, 120, 121, 122, 123, 127a, 127b, 131, 134, 135, 136, 140, 141, 142, 143, 146, 160, 162, 163, 169
DIRECÇÃO REGIONAL TURISMO DA MADEIRA 72, 101, 171, 183
DREAMSTIME.COM/Emacojocaru 5
FLICKR/denvilles duo 25, 92; ahisgett 61, 71b; Madeira 161
GORDON LETHBRIDGE 1, 31, 42, 54, 65, 73, 77, 91, 95, 107, 111, 117, 139, 155, 175
MARC DI DUCA 12, 19, 26, 46, 47, 85, 98, 102, 103, 126, 137, 167, 184
PICTURES COLOUR LIBRARY 70, 129, 149
SPECTRUM COLOUR LIBRARY 13, 22, 23, 80
WIKIMEDIA COMMONS/Adriao 17
WORLD PICTURES/PHOTOSHOT 27, 48, 147, 151, 152, 153, 164

For CAMBRIDGE PUBLISHING MANAGEMENT LTD:
Project editor: Diane Teillol
Typesetter: Trevor Double/Paul Queripel
Proofreader and indexer: Karolin Thomas

SEND YOUR THOUGHTS TO
BOOKS@THOMASCOOK.COM

We're committed to providing the very best up-to-date information in our travel guides and constantly strive to make them as useful as they can be. You can help us to improve future editions by letting us have your feedback. If you've made a wonderful discovery on your travels that we don't already feature, if you'd like to inform us about recent changes to anything that we do include, or if you simply want to let us know your thoughts about this guidebook and how we can make it even better – we'd love to hear from you.

Send us ideas, discoveries and recommendations today and then look out for your valuable input in the next edition of this title.

Emails to the above address, or letters to traveller guides Series Editor, Thomas Cook Publishing, PO Box 227, Coningsby Road, Peterborough PE3 8SB, UK.

Please don't forget to let us know which title your feedback refers to!